"Scott Symington tackles an important topic that affects almost 20 percent of all people at any given time—anxiety. In this easy-to-read book, he guides the reader through an innovative approach called the Two-Screen Method, where we learn how to deal with worries visually, and apply mindfulness principles when we need it the most. Through specific steps and well-told client stories, the readers are provided with a blueprint to ease themselves from their own anxious patterns and break the loop of fears that hold them back from achieving advancement, peace, and better relationships. A must-read for anyone!"

—**Karen J. Miller, PhD**, clinical neuropsychologist and health sciences professor at the University of California, Los Angeles

"It is rare that a new book actually presents a truly new thought, perspective, or tool. Scott Symington's *Freedom from Anxious Thoughts and Feelings* does all three; his groundbreaking Two-Screen Method for dealing with anxiety is broadly applicable and effective. We use his approach regularly in working with clients who are struggling with sexual issues. We find it is a tool that people can easily visualize and apply in order to accept, but put aside, interfering emotions while focusing on and pursuing spiritually sound, relationship-enhancing, and life-giving goals."

—**Clifford** and **Joyce Penner**, sexual therapists, educators, and authors of *The Gift of Sex*

"Scott Symington's remarkable book is apt to enhance the emotional well-being of anyone who simply reads it through carefully one time. For those who wish to gain the best possible benefit of the book, he provides the tools. This is no theoretical work or an extended sales pitch for starting therapy. Symington is confident that most readers who suffer from anxiety, worry, or depression will significantly enhance the quality of their inner lives by diligently following his Two-Screen Method guidelines for about twelve weeks. He makes a convincing case and offers tremendous hope in an overly stressed world."

—**Anthony J. Mulkern, PhD**, president of Mulkern Associates

"Scott Symington's Two-Screen Method combines several years of clinical therapeutic experience with the practical skills of mindfulness training to provide a process that creates internal psychological space within the person, which allows for the growth and development that permits us to be free of anxious thoughts and feelings. This method visually guides us toward self-acceptance by challenging distorted views of our identity, so that we can live in the present moment and find our true self and ultimate value."

—**James A. Van Slyke, PhD**, associate professor in the
department of psychology at Fresno Pacific University,
and author of *The Cognitive Science of Religion*

"Scott Symington has done a masterful and creative job in synthesizing psychological research and clinical practice into a book that is relatable, easy to understand, practical, and easy to apply. I wholeheartedly recommend this book to both therapists and their clients, as well as anyone interested in acquiring effective tools for dealing with anxiety. Indeed, freedom from problematic anxious thoughts and feelings is possible. I expect many lives will be profoundly impacted by this book."

—**Paul Lo, PhD**, clinical psychologist and chief of the
Mental Health Clinic Section at the VA Greater
Los Angeles Healthcare System, Los Angeles, CA

"Scott Symington uses captivating imagery to not just tell, but vividly *show* how to change your relationship with anxiety. The two-step approach in this book is a powerful way to evade the clutches of anxiety, and then use the momentum to experience life more deeply and take action to live your best life. I personally use this practice regularly and teach it to my clients who are delighted by how simple and profound it is."

—**Jeanette Lantz, PhD, BCB**, founder and director
of Cognitive Behavior Therapy Northwest

"Living as we do in a world of fear and anxiety, Scott Symington gives us a powerful tool to face, accept, and move beyond these pervasive forces inside and around us. This book is a practical, realistic, and transformative guide. Read it, practice it, and find freedom."

—**Mark Labberton, PhD, MDiv**, president of Fuller Theological Seminary

"With this book, Scott Symington shares the secrets he has unlocked through years of real-world clinical experience with a wide variety of anxious clients. A unique combination of time-tested therapeutic techniques coupled with innovative practices, his Two-Screen Method is a valuable addition to the cognitive behavioral therapy tool chest. The easy-to-follow explanations and recommendations will open readers up to a world of sweet relief as they move through the steps and shed the fears that have held them hostage. As you climb the Freedom Ladder, prepare to trade in your exhausting anxieties for a new set of positive, life-affirming beliefs that will carry you forward into a happier ever after."

—**Susanne Whatley**, news host on NPR affiliate KPCC in Los Angeles, CA

FREEDOM
FROM
ANXIOUS
THOUGHTS &
FEELINGS

A TWO-STEP MINDFULNESS APPROACH
FOR MOVING BEYOND FEAR & WORRY

SCOTT SYMINGTON, PhD

NEW HARBINGER PUBLICATIONS, INC.

Publisher's Note

This publication is designed to provide accurate and authoritative information in regard to the subject matter covered. It is sold with the understanding that the publisher is not engaged in rendering psychological, financial, legal, or other professional services. If expert assistance or counseling is needed, the services of a competent professional should be sought.

Distributed in Canada by Raincoast Books

Copyright © 2019 by Scott Symington
New Harbinger Publications, Inc.
5674 Shattuck Avenue
Oakland, CA 94609
www.newharbinger.com

Cover design by Amy Shoup

Acquired by Jess O'Brien

Edited by Kristi Hein

All Rights Reserved

Library of Congress Cataloging-in-Publication Data on file

21   20   19

10   9   8   7   6   5   4   3   2   1   First Printing

CONTENTS

WHAT DO I DO INSIDE MY HEAD?

Prominently displayed in our family room is a quote from St. Irenaeus of Lyons: "The Glory of God is the human person fully alive." I love this quote. It speaks to our design. It helps us understand the restlessness of the human spirit—that part of self that refuses to be contained or muted. Inside us all, whether conscious or unconscious, is a burning desire to burst out onto life's stage, proclaiming, "Here I am!" It's the human person fully alive.

As a clinical psychologist in full-time private practice, I have a front-row seat on those influences that cripple the human spirit, blocking people from a life fully lived—chronic worrying, depressed moods, destructive patterns of behavior. In the midst of these struggles, everything may look fine on the outside. You might see a smile or all the trappings of success. But looks can be deceiving. On the inside, these people can feel embattled or hopeless or out of control. They feel trapped by and stuck with thoughts, feelings, and behaviors they don't understand and can't seem to change.

Take Laura, for example, who feels anxious in social situations. Following a conversation or social interaction, she's regularly plagued by worries of having said something "stupid" or others laughing behind her back. Then there's Emma, who's prone to depressed moods. A Facebook post or news of a friend's engagement can automatically trigger painful thoughts of comparison: *Why don't I have a boyfriend? Why does everyone else get to enjoy life except for me?* As she travels down memory lane, recalling times when she felt hurt and rejected, her mood and outlook on life darken.

With Gary, it's less about emotional pain and more about a behavior he can't control. Dozens of times he's promised his wife—and himself—that he'll stop looking at internet pornography. Most of the time it's not a struggle for him to stick to this commitment. Then, before he knows it, especially during stressful seasons at work, he falls back into the same unwanted pattern.

All these individuals are stuck in patterns of thought, emotional reactions, and behaviors that cause pain and problems in their lives. They find themselves in this predicament not because they lack the desire or willpower to change—just the opposite. They want nothing more than to enjoy and feel good about the life they're living. Which makes sense—who wants to be up at 2:00 a.m. stuck in a worry loop? What's attractive about a depressed mood or a repetitive behavior that puts in jeopardy an important relationship or deeply held value?

Lacking the desire or intention to change is not the issue. In these situations, our struggle is with knowing what to do on the inside to change the way we're thinking, feeling, or acting. We're not clear on what to do with our thoughts or how to respond to the feelings to shift our experience. No matter what we try, we often find ourselves back in the same feeling, chewing on the same recycled worries, repeating the same unhealthy behavior.

This tendency to get and remain stuck shouldn't come as a surprise. After all, we've never been taught how thoughts and feelings work. Though the quality of our life is greatly determined by how we feel on the inside, we've being going through life without an internal map or guide. Our primary education has been about expanding our knowledge of the external world—how things work on the outside. Somehow, we all missed the course titled *Navigating Your Internal World 101*. We've been trying to live a free and meaningful life without even the basic knowledge of how to prevent ourselves from being overrun by a feeling or protect our mind from the thought patterns that fuel negative moods and unhealthy behaviors. We've been left to fend for ourselves in our mental and emotional life.

To make matters worse, the actions we do take, in the absence of an internal map or guide, often exacerbate the negative symptom or pattern. Our reflexive responses and natural ways of coping with internal challenges—the anxious feeling, the destructive urge, the negative mood—end up fueling the very internal activity we're trying to defuse.

Unaware that the psychological realm is a universe unto itself, filled with paradoxes and counterintuitive principles, we apply the problem-solving methods that seem to work in our daily lives to challenges showing up in our minds and emotions. We study and analyze perceived threats (anxious worries). We run from— or try to fight off—sources of pain or fear. We take steps to establish a sense of safety and security. And the list goes on.

But all these strategies backfire. The more we try to seek emotional safety or change the way we're feeling or get rid of threatening thoughts, the more we energize the unwanted thoughts and feelings. Our natural, reflexive internal responses end up empowering the very thoughts and feelings from which we're seeking freedom.

To break free from the current pattern, you need to relate to thoughts and feelings—especially the problematic ones—in a new way. Certain internal reactions support the thoughts and feelings coming into our awareness, while other responses cause them to dissipate. When the worry comes into your mind—when the challenging feelings show up—you need to know the specific internal action steps that will decrease their power and presence.

That's what this book is about. You'll be introduced to a powerful, easy-to-use method for de-energizing and breaking free from anxious thoughts and destructive feelings. It's called the Two-Screen Method® (TSM).

The Two-Screen Method

What makes the Two-Screen Method unique—and especially helpful—is how it, in the words of one client, shows you "what to do inside your head." Instead of describing and giving you instructions on how to stop worrying or get emotional relief, TSM actually guides you—on the inside—through the mental and emotional steps that lead to the desired change. What makes this possible is the novel way you're taken through the change process. Your companion and guide is an image inside your mind. You imagine your internal world as a media room with two screens. On the wall you see facing forward is the *front screen*, which represents the present moment and life-giving internal activity—all the thoughts, feelings, and images that translate into well-being and a life well lived. Off to the right, still inside your mind, is a *side screen*—the place where the fears, worries, unhealthy urges, and destructive moods show up. With this image in mind, you are then shown how to de-energize the problematic thoughts and feelings showing up on the side screen, while cultivating your ability to be in the present moment and express the best parts of who you are on the front screen.

This visual approach allows you to take advantage of some of the most effective psychological strategies, simply by relating to the image in your mind as directed. More specifically, TSM enables you to access and apply mindfulness principles with ease. You may or may not be familiar with the term *mindfulness* or be aware of the explosion of mindfulness-based treatments in the field of psychology. We'll talk more about mindfulness later, especially in chapter 4, but for now simply know that mindfulness is a way of relating to your inner and outer experience with an attitude of openness, acceptance, and present-moment focus. As you become more mindful, as you learn to be more accepting of challenging feelings and more tolerant of alarming thoughts coming into awareness, these sources of pain that you struggle with become less powerful inside you.

Resolving the Translation Problem

The challenge with mindfulness—or any treatment approach, for that matter—is knowing how to apply the helpful principles and strategies to your life. It's one thing to understand a psychological theory or idea on an intellectual level; it's quite another to actually follow the recommendation in the midst of intense anxiety or a destructive urge—to figure out the specific steps you need to take. Let's say you feel anxious in this moment. Ideally, you want to accept the presence of the anxious feeling without dwelling on it or making it the focus of your attention. You want to apply the principle of acceptance to your anxious experience, creating space for and accepting the presence of unwanted thoughts and feelings—a defining feature of mindfulness. When you take this mindful approach, the anxiety or internal challenge will lose its power and dissipate.

But what exactly does *acceptance* mean? Acceptance is just a word, a concept. What does it actually look like inside your mind? What specific mental and emotional steps embody this idea of acceptance? When two separate worlds—the external world of language and psychological concepts and the internal world of thoughts and feelings—try to communicate, much gets lost in translation. Even when you do your best to follow the recommended strategy, you never know for sure whether you're actually applying it to your experience. As a result, you can miss out on using interventions that can relieve suffering and improve your quality of life, getting the help you need.

This is where the Two-Screen Method comes in. It doesn't require you to convert verbal directions and theoretical concepts into internal action steps. Instead, the principles and steps that lead to freedom are communicated visually. TSM guides you through the change process—through the world of thoughts and feelings—visually and spatially. TSM gives you an intuitive image that naturally structures your internal experience, so you can see what is happening and what you need to do to get the relief you

desire. The core tasks of mindfulness and other empirically supported strategies are communicated and applied simply by relating to the image of two screens as directed. This resolves the
translation problem, making helpful psychological concepts and
strategies easily accessible and applicable to your struggle. This
boosts your ability to break free from the current pattern and shift
your experience in times of need—when you are feeling most
anxious or negative.

A Path Toward Freedom and Aliveness

In this book, you'll discover what to do on the inside to experience greater levels of mental and emotional freedom. You'll learn
how the image of two screens can free your mind from worry and
take the energy out of a destructive feeling. In addition, beyond
addressing an identified problem or current struggle, the Two-
Screen Method is designed to enhance your quality of life. In the
following pages, you'll encounter ways to tap into unexpressed
parts of yourself, get important needs met, and inject more aliveness into your life. In fact, the TSM side screen activity, such as
an anxious or insecure feeling or an unhealthy craving, is linked
to and used as a springboard for positive action. The presence of
an anxious thought becomes a reminder to help or encourage
someone in need. The energy from internal agitation and anxious
feelings is redirected into healthy activities, such as physical exercise, creative tasks, and other sources of aliveness. In other words,
if you dig in and fully apply the content in this book, you can do
more than resolve the issue of concern. You can positively move
your life forward and take steps to more fully express the best
parts of who you are. This is the greatest of victories—when you
take a problem or source of pain and use it to build a more fulfilling and meaningful life.

CHAPTER 1

SEEING YOUR INTERNAL WORLD
Introducing the Two-Screen Method

The time is fast approaching. In a few minutes Nathan will stand up and give a toast at his grandmother's ninetieth birthday party. He feels the nervous energy. He contemplates dashing off to the restroom for one last run-through, even though he committed the toast to memory weeks ago. Nathan catches himself. He recognizes what's happening and what he needs to do. He reminds himself not to go away in his mind, but instead to accept the anxious feeling.

Soon friends and relatives take a seat at one of the tables spread across the backyard. Nathan's sister stands up to give the first toast. Nathan knows he's next. He feels the adrenaline surging through his body. His heart pounds and his breath quickens. Nathan tries to stay loose and takes medium-sized breaths as he leans forward with his mental attention. His mind naturally wants to think about his toast and manage what he's feeling. In response to this inward pull, Nathan hooks his attention on his sister, hanging on each word she speaks. This intense focus on his sister's toast not only protects Nathan from giving his attention to the nervous feeling but also supports his values—what he really cares about in the moment. He's there to celebrate his grandmother. Nathan wants to be present and engaged with the experience, which includes actually listening to what's shared.

When it's Nathan's turn, his body is on high alert. He reminds himself to accept the experience of being afraid. As he stands up, he feels anxious, but he's not consumed by it. It's there but it doesn't take over, almost as if he is riding on top of the anxious feeling. He finds his grandmother's face in the crowd. As they lock eyes, everything is put into perspective. *This moment,* he thinks to himself, *is so much bigger than whatever I'm feeling.* Nathan raises his glass and offers words of love and gratitude. After he sits down, several at the table nod and smile and express how they were touched by his words. He still feels the nervous energy, but it dissipates with each passing moment. He resists the temptation to review the mental tapes of what just happened or elicit reassurance from others at the table. He focuses on staying in the present moment, and a few minutes later he begins to relax and feel internally settled.

When Nathan recounted this experience in a recent therapy session, I couldn't hold back a smile. This represented a break-through. In his first major test since beginning treatment, he'd been able to successfully apply the Two-Screen Method. That's not to say it was an easy experience for Nathan. Feeling anxious is never easy, even when you handle it well. This was true for Nathan too. He had to contend with waves of anxious physical sensations (heart pounding, shallow breathing, and so on) and stay on top of a mind that wanted to turn inward and chase after worries. Despite these challenges, at no point did the anxiety take over. He handled the event with grace, poise, and psychological wisdom. He stayed anchored and connected to his values through-out the experience. It was a sign that Nathan's relationship to the anxiety was changing. The collection of worrisome thoughts and anxious feelings that had banded together to give expression to his debilitating social anxiety and fear of public speaking were beginning to lose their grip on his life.

If Nathan stays on the current path, anxiety will become increasingly less present in his life, in terms of both frequency and intensity.

This idea of having a relationship with thoughts and feelings is key to understanding how changes like Nathan's can occur. There are the thoughts that come into your mind and the feelings that rise up inside you, and then there is your pattern of responses to this internal activity. These thoughts and feelings—especially the unwelcome ones—are a part of you, but they don't define you. You are not the worry. You are not the anxious feeling. These are experiences showing up inside you, but they don't speak to who you are, what you believe, or what you decide to do in life.

There's a sacred space that exists in your internal world, between the challenging thoughts and feelings coming into awareness and your core self or center—a center that can sit back and observe internal activity. In this critical space—the gap between your internal observer and the surrounding thoughts and feelings—you have the freedom to make choices. You can hang out and invest in the worry, or you can find an alternative home for your attention. You can fight the emotional pain or adopt a different attitude to the internal challenge. You can allow what you're currently feeling to dictate what you will and won't do today, or you can assume a leadership position, making choices that align with your values and the life you desire.

How you respond to these internal challenges will determine your psychological freedom and well-being. This is true because what you do on the inside—what you do with your mind, how you respond emotionally and behaviorally—will either breathe life into the anxious experience or cause it to dissipate.

Ideally, you want to follow Nathan's example, accepting the anxious thoughts and feelings without making them the focus of your attention. You allow the unwanted thoughts and feelings to run their course, but you keep your mind focused on the task at hand, the present moment, or an activity that aligns with your values. By following this strategy, you cut off anxiety's oxygen supply and experience a new level of psychological freedom and well-being.

The challenge is to take this strategy, which sounds good and promises to be helpful, and actually apply it to the worries and other barriers to happiness present in your life. That's what the Two-Screen Method is designed to do. It uses the image of two screens to guide you through the specific mental and emotional steps that free you from anxious worries and other threats to well-being.

The Two Screens

Imagine your internal world as a media room with two screens. All possible thoughts, feelings, and physical sensations show up in this room on one of two screens. On the wall you see facing forward is the primary or front screen. This is the place where the positive and life-giving thoughts, feelings, and images show up. It's the home of joy, contentment, and connection. It's looking into the face of a loved one, attending to the present moment, being in a flow at work, laughing with a friend, feeling spiritually connected, and expressing the best parts of who you are. It's the experience of being fully present, feeling alive, and living out deeply held values. It's all the inner activity that gives you a sense of well-being. When you say to yourself, *Today is a good day*, it's a sign you've been connected to the front screen.

Consciously or unconsciously, we're all trying to stay connected to the front screen.

The challenge is, off to the right is a side screen competing for your attention. This is the place where the threats, fears, anxieties, unhealthy temptations, and potentially destructive thoughts and feelings show up. You will be in a conversation, on the way to work, or trying to sleep when suddenly the side screen lights up and your internal eyes reflexively swivel over to take a look. Scrolling across the screen, there's an anxious thought or unsettling image.

If you sit there and watch the side screen for too long, you risk becoming ensnared. It doesn't take much exposure before you get caught up in the worries or seduced by the destructive urge or mood. This happens because the side screen uses your preoccupied attention and reactivity as an energy source. Under the spotlight of attention, the destructive mood or anxious feeling intensifies. The images become more colorful and pronounced. The sound gets louder. Before long the side screen is IMAX theater quality with Dolby surround sound, and you've lost your ability to rotate back to the front screen.

Let's be clear here: you can't control what shows up on the side screen. Nor can you control the reflexive swivel of your attention when the unwanted thoughts and feelings first come into awareness. You will suddenly find yourself gazing at an anxious idea or depressive image scrolling across the screen. It's what you do next that's important.

You'll be tempted to watch, analyze, debate, fight, or run from the thoughts, feelings, and physical sensations announcing themselves on the side screen. All these responses may be natural, but they keep the side screen shining brightly. The more you try to avoid or resist an anxious feeling, the stronger it becomes. The longer you study the worry or entertain memories of past failures, the more anxious and down you'll feel—and so on.

To be free—to get the relief you're seeking—you need to relate to the side screen in a new way that deprives it of your attention and reactivity. If you remove the spotlight of attention and purge the system of reactivity (efforts at resisting the unwanted experience), you pull the plug on the side screen's energy source, causing it to fade into the background.

How the Method Works

The Two-Screen Method shows you how to put these ideas into practice in two steps: striking a new relationship with the side screen, and staying anchored to the front screen.

A New Response to Challenging Thoughts and Feelings

Ideally, you want to cultivate a relationship with the side screen that is defined by acceptance and nonresistance. When an anxious thought or feeling announces itself—*I'm going to make a fool of myself*—your internal eyes will automatically dart over to the side screen, where the image of yourself being horribly embarrassed might be playing. As soon as you realize you're on the side screen, with your new awareness you are guided by the motto *accept and redirect*. You accept the hard feelings or unanswered questions, while gently redirecting your attention back to the front screen.

As you plant your attention on the front screen, you allow the side screen to run its tape in your peripheral vision. You accept the distracting stream of thoughts and images, as well as the emotional heat being kicked off the side screen. You accept the experience of being heckled or taunted from the sidelines—*I'm going to fail, I'll be a laughingstock.* Acceptance doesn't mean you like or agree with the content of the side screen. The thoughts and feelings displayed there may be aversive or contrary to what you believe or what you want to have happen. Acceptance is about letting go internally, focusing on what you can control, and responding to the unwanted thoughts and feelings with psychological wisdom. You move into acceptance and nonresistance, even though it goes against your instincts, because this is the opposite of reactivity. It's the response that cuts off the side screen's energy source, ultimately freeing you from the anxious feeling or destructive mood.

In summary, the first step in the Two-Screen Method is reshaping your relationship with the side screen, de-energizing the problematic thoughts and feelings by applying mindfulness principles. Mindfulness, again, is a particular way of being and orientation toward the thoughts and feelings showing up inside you. As it's practiced and applied in psychology, mindfulness is focused on increasing your ability to be in the present moment, while maintaining a disposition of acceptance and nonresistance toward the thoughts, feelings, and physical sensations coming into awareness—especially the challenging and unwanted thoughts and feelings. The second step is learning how to stay connected to the front screen, using one or more of the three primary anchors that are designed to hold your attention as you're redirecting away from the side screen: Mindfulness Skills, Healthy Distractions and Activities, and Loving Action.

The side screen will frequently exert a strong pull on your mind. During these times, it's often not realistic to say, "Don't watch!" unless you have another home for your attention with some sticking power. That's where the front screen anchors come in. These anchors give you a safe place to anchor your attention while the side screen storm is passing through. But this is not all they do. The front screen anchors are also designed to grow you as a person and enhance your quality of life. They help you take the energy that is normally consumed by the side screen and redirect it to activities that cultivate a sense of aliveness and well-being.

Using the Front Screen Anchors

The first anchor designed to hold your attention on the front screen, Mindfulness Skills, is focused on increasing your capacity to be in the present moment. It's helpful to think of mindfulness—your ability to be attuned to the present moment—as a muscle set that needs to be developed. Right now, you may find it difficult to keep your mind in the present moment, but if you exercise these mindfulness muscles on a regular basis, they'll become strong and available to help in times of need, when you're prone to worry or vulnerable to a depressed mood. Conversely, if you neglect these muscles, they will atrophy—or never develop—and you'll miss out on an important source of well-being and help.

TSM takes a practical and targeted approach to building and sustaining this muscle set. You're given a series of streamlined mindfulness exercises that are easy to practice and integrate into a busy life. Some of this mindfulness training involves approaching ordinary tasks of life, such as driving or washing the dishes, with the intention of present-moment awareness: the designated activity is engaged with all five senses (sight, hearing, touch, taste, and smell). These experiences not only cultivate a mindful disposition toward inner activity—helping you be less controlled by problematic thoughts and feelings—but also allow you to plumb the richness of fully showing up in the present moment. That's something most of us don't often do.

The chapter on mindfulness skills also offers strategies for challenging moments—when you're caught in an endless cycle of worry or feel emotionally overwhelmed. During these times, it's not uncommon to be consumed by the side screen and, despite your best efforts, be unable to rotate to the front screen. To address this challenge, you'll learn a powerful mindfulness technique that rapidly and effectively brings your mind into the present moment, drawing your internal eyes to the front screen. As you'll read later, you can't be worrying or investing in a destructive mood and be in the present moment. These ruminative internal activities, which are the equivalent to watching the side screen, are neurologically incompatible with present-moment awareness. When you have a reliable way of bringing your mind into the here and now, you also have a way to exit worry loops and gain healthy space from destructive moods.

All of the exercises that fall under the Mindfulness Skills anchor increase your capacity to focus attention on your chosen object. As you begin implementing TSM, you may need to actively and repeatedly redirect away from the side screen. It's a process: whenever you catch yourself watching the side screen, you patiently redirect back to the present moment. As you become more consistent with this pattern of redirecting, you actually make changes in your brain that strengthen your ability to direct and sustain attention on the location of your choice. Your consistent efforts in redirecting attention to the front screen encourage the development of new *neural pathways*—neurons (nerve cells) that band together to form the equivalent of an information superhighway in the brain, sending signals from one region to another.

The second anchor designed to keep you tethered to the front screen is Healthy Distractions and Activities (HDAs). HDAs are various physical, pleasurable, and enlivening activities that offer a safe home for your attention and life energy. When you're particularly challenged by the side screen, in the midst of an anxious experience or painful feeling, it may feel like a gravitational pull on your mind and person. The insecure or threatening feelings scrolling across the screen scream for your attention, and you feel compelled to unpack them. That's when the HDA anchor can tether your internal eyes to the front screen with a healthy distraction or activity, protecting you from being drawn in and preoccupied with the side screen content, which only strengthens the destructive thoughts and feelings. In chapter 6 you will be guided through an exercise to identify a list of activities that are effective tethers for your mind. After accepting and turning your attention away from the worry you may, for example, spend ten minutes reading an engaging novel or working on the family jigsaw puzzle. You remove the side screen's power by letting it play its tape off to the right, as you attend to the external activity on the front screen.

But the HDA anchor can function as more than just a way to steer yourself away from the side screen. As you'll discover, you can channel your life energy into an activity that taps into your creative side or improves your health or gives you an injection of aliveness. Chapter 6 shows you how to enhance your quality of life while you're mindfully moving away from the negative thoughts and feelings crackling on the side screen.

The third and final anchor is Loving Action—expressions of support, care, and kindness that often tap into deeply held values and express the best parts of who we are. These types of actions are a powerful and counterintuitive response to side screen activity. When we feel anxious or are visited by a destructive mood or urge, we're often not thinking of others. We become self-focused and preoccupied with resolving our insecurities or managing our own pain. In these spaces, it's easy to lose sight of what's important and who we want to be.

The Loving Action anchor disrupts this cycle by turning it on its head. You'll learn how to use side screen activity, such as a threatening thought or an anxious feeling, as an internal reminder to encourage or pray for someone else or engage in an act of kindness toward yourself or another person. The Loving Action anchor offers the opportunity and satisfaction of using side screen energy—which has had a destructive influence in your life—as a tailwind to express the best parts of who you are and what you believe.

You can use these three front screen anchors by themselves or collectively, depending on what is most helpful to you. They're designed to keep you in the present moment (Mindfulness Skills), find a safe home for your attention and life energy (Healthy Distractions and Activities), and convert challenging experiences—your side screen activity—into opportunities to express the best of who you are (Loving Action).

And that, in a nutshell, is the Two-Screen Method.

Conclusion

The image of two screens that we've been exploring—the front screen representing present-moment experience and all that is enriching and life-giving, and the side screen showing the destructive, anxious, worried, and fearful thoughts and images that inevitably capture our attention and take us away from the present moment—transforms the highly complex abstraction of your internal world into something concrete and understandable. With the two screens, you're given a clear picture of what's happening, what to do, and what not to do. You can understand the problem and see the solution. Best of all, this method shows you what to do on the inside to make the change, rather than leaving you to figure it out. Like so many others who have used the Two-Screen Method, you can gain freedom from anxious worries, destructive moods, and other barriers to happiness through this straightforward process of accepting what appears on the side screen while hooking your attention to the front screen.

With that, let's begin.

CHAPTER 2

UNDERSTANDING YOUR ANXIOUS SIDE SCREEN

What do you worry about? What makes you anxious? What fears do you struggle with?

The anxious side screen has an endless supply of psychological threats designed to hook your attention. You may be at work, or lying in bed, or driving your car, or in the middle of a conversation, when the anxious side screen lights up: *Did I turn off the stove before I left? I know that test today is going to be a hard one; what if I fail? Oh man, here comes that freeway overpass I hate...* When it does, you reflexively turn inward and begin watching the worrisome thoughts and images scrolling across the side screen: thoughts of your house burning down because of your negligence; a dread that you'll fail that test and your life will be ruined; the image of a car spiraling out of control on the overpass, bringing your life to a horrible end.

These thoughts and images hold your attention because it feels like something you value, something you care about, is at risk. As you watch, study, analyze, and wrestle with the perceived threats, the anxious feelings intensify and you are drawn deeper into the side screen. All the while, on the front screen a productive and meaningful life passes you by.

The goal of this chapter, as well as the one that follows, is to help you break free from the anxious side screen so you're less controlled and preoccupied with life-choking worries and anxious feelings. We'll begin by exploring the mental, emotional, and behavioral reactions that energize anxiety. Once you understand what keeps the worries and anxious feelings going, you'll be shown a new way of relating to the anxious side screen—to anxiety—that will give you the freedom and relief you're seeking.

To set the stage for our journey, let's clarify the type of thoughts and feelings that show up on your side screen.

What Are Fear and Anxiety?

Broadly defined, fear and anxiety are the experience of being under threat. They are what you think and feel when the threat center—that part of your brain assigned the critical task of keeping you safe and protecting what you value—sounds the alarm, alerting you to danger. The threat center grabs your attention in two primary ways. First, when it senses you could be harmed physically, it activates the well-known fight-or-flight response. When this is triggered, adrenaline and cortisol are immediately pumped into your body, your muscles contract, and blood flows to regions of the body that will help you either fight, to neutralize the threat, or take flight, to escape the danger.

To illustrate, imagine you're on a camping trip and decide to take shelter in a cave. In the middle of the night, you wake up and see a grizzly bear in the cave. Instantly, you feel fear. You're hit with a wave of panic and sense of impending doom. Your heart rate goes wild, you sweat profusely, and your body is ready to run a hundred miles per hour. Thoughts also flash through your mind: *I'm going to die! I don't want my life to end this way!* And depending on how much time you have before you must act, you may even engage in some basic problem solving: *Should I play dead or run?*

You can also have a fear experience that is less about immediate danger and more about future possibilities or the sense that something you care about is at risk—how others see you, financial security, being a good parent, successfully completing a work project, the well-being of loved ones, and so on. This is the second way the threat center can operate in your life. It's an experience of fear that tends to be less intense physiologically and involves more thoughts—lots of thinking. You mentally study and analyze the concern. You imagine potential scenarios and think through ways you could protect what you care about. The feeling part of fear—the physiological and emotional experience—is still present, but usually at a lower level than with the fight-or-flight response. Here's an example:

Let's say your nineteen-year-old son is driving to the mountains with a friend this weekend. A couple of days before the trip, you're on your computer and see snow forecast for the area he's traveling to. Immediately, you have thoughts about your son's safety. *He doesn't know how to drive in the snow! If he goes on this trip, I'll be an anxious wreck all weekend!* While you prefer that he stay home, you know making this demand wouldn't go over well—you're not even sure you would prevail. You begin problem solving, trying to minimize the perceived threat. *What can I do?* You remember there are tire chains in the garage and that your spouse's car has front-wheel drive, which is best for snow conditions. You also decide to respectfully ask your son to watch a YouTube tutorial on driving in the snow. As you take action to address your concerns, your anxious experience becomes contained and manageable.

Your Brain Overestimates Threats

In these two illustrations, you may have noticed that there was no mention of maladaptive anxiety: the experience of being afraid or worrying when the threat is imagined or improbable or completely outside your control. Whether it was reacting to the grizzly or preparing your son for snow conditions, your threat center was, for the most part, doing its job and serving you well; fear helped you respond adaptively to the situation. As you probably know from personal experience, however, this is not always the case. Your threat center can cause you to worry and feel anxious unnecessarily. The same fear response you have when threatened by a bear can get triggered by speaking in public or entering a crowded elevator. The same anxiety that can help you solve problems and conscientiously manage your life responsibilities can attach itself to ideas and imagined scenarios where there's no real identifiable threat or concern.

This happens because the threat center of your brain errs on the side of overestimating risk. It would rather falsely sound the alarm than miss a genuine threat. And when it does sound the alarm, even if you're not in danger, even if the worry has no basis in reality or is not worthy of your attention, you have the same mental, emotional, and physical experience of being under threat. Your threat center doesn't distinguish between *possible* threat and *certain* threat. It either pulls the trigger—announcing the threat and giving you a fear experience—or it doesn't. Understandably, in the midst of your anxious experience, this can make it difficult to differentiate between legitimate threats that you should pay attention to and those concerns that *feel* real but are really just psychological threats and recycled worries in disguise.

Understanding Your Anxious Side Screen

As we explore your anxious experience, it's important to distinguish between the adaptive anxiety that helps us and the life-constricting type that shows up on the side screen. When I use the terms *fear*, *worry*, and *anxiety* in this book, I don't mean the healthy fear that protects you from physical harm in an emergency situation, or the healthy anxiety that functions as a useful internal alarm, reminding you to pay the overdue bill or finalize plans for the upcoming trip so things run smoothly. This type of fear is healthy. We want to listen to it. It keeps us safe and helps us live a responsible, even moral life.

In this chapter, we're addressing the destructive type of fear—the anxiety and worry that prevents you from finding rest and living a full life. This type of fear, the anxiety that shows up on the side screen, is a life constrictor. Unlike constructive anxiety, it adds no value to your life. It serves no purpose. It leads people to avoid planes, elevators, the doctor's office, social situations, and even the outdoors. It makes you preoccupied and afraid when there's no real danger. It tangles your mind up with recycled worries about what people think, the uncertainty of the future, and the potential loss of someone or something you care about. It causes you to withdraw into your head to fight battles that can't be won and analyze problems that can't be solved. In the meantime, you miss out on being fully present and engaged with your life.

As we just discussed, however, it's not easy to ignore the experience of feeling under threat. Even if part of you senses that your anxious experience or worry is overstated, it still *feels* real, making it hard to separate legitimate worries from the harmful kind.

To help you distinguish healthy anxiety from destructive anxiety—the anxious thoughts and feelings showing up on your side screen—it's helpful to look at the pattern. Ask yourself the simple question: *Is this something I tend to worry about?* If the worry or anxiety matches a repeating theme, such as perpetually worrying about disappointing others or losing a loved one, you can treat the concern, at least in the short term, as a psychological threat showing up on your side screen rather than a genuine threat requiring immediate attention and problem solving.

I once treated a client with health fears who had a pattern of visiting medical specialists to rule out a long list of feared diseases and illnesses. Time and time again she was found to be in good health. As she left the doctor's office with the reassuring news, she would feel a deep sense of relief. But this respite didn't last long. The next unfamiliar symptom or physical discomfort reignited her fears. In treatment, she worked on connecting the health concern of the moment to the historical pattern of anxiety that consumed her life. For example, when she developed a headache, which activated her fear of a brain tumor, she learned to pause and ask herself if the current fear fit her pattern of worry. When it did, she reminded herself not to analyze or problem solve the perceived fear for at least twenty-four hours. This was an important first step in breaking the anxious cycle—stepping back and seeing whether her anxious experience conformed to a recurring theme and profile.

When you can recognize your fear patterns, you'll be more able to stay focused on the front screen and tend to what's happening in the here and now, instead of worrying about an idle threat that keeps you from living your life.

MY ANXIOUS SIDE SCREEN

What are the recurring anxious themes showing up in your life? What tends to trigger these fears? How would you describe your anxious experience, in terms of thoughts, feelings, images, and bodily sensations? To develop an accurate picture of your anxiety, complete the "My Anxious Side Screen" form. (A worksheet for this form is available at http://www.newharbinger.com/42327.)

Anxious Triggers	
Anxious Thoughts	
Anxious Feelings	
Bodily Sensations	
Anxious Images	

Anxiety's Three Sources of Energy

Now that we've clarified the type of worries and fears that can populate your side screen, we want to work on removing anxiety's power and presence in your life. The first step toward a non-anxious life begins with understanding how anxiety—especially destructive anxiety—is energized. You need to know the mental, emotional, and behavioral movements that fuel the anxious symptoms. As depicted in figure 2.1, the anxious side screen draws its energy from three sources:

Spotlight of Attention: the mental focus we place on worries and anxious feelings

Reactivity: the way we resist or try to fight anxious thoughts and feelings

Avoidance Behaviors: the way we avoid situations that activate the anxious side screen

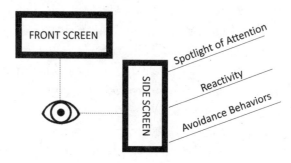

Figure 2.1: Anxiety's Three Sources of Energy

In this next section, we'll explore how the spotlight of attention, reactivity, and avoidance behaviors intensify the worries and anxious feelings showing up on your side screen. This will set the stage for the next chapter, which shows you how to deprive your side screen—and the related anxious thoughts and feelings—of these three energy sources.

The First Source of Energy: The Spotlight of Attention

What you see looking directly ahead is your front screen. It's the present moment—what you're experiencing right now. It's also all those internal experiences—those thoughts, feelings, and images—associated with well-being and living a full, vibrant life, whether that's having a flow experience at work, conversing or laughing with a friend, or taking a relaxing walk around the neighborhood. When you're connected to the front screen, life may not be perfect, but you basically feel content and settled internally.

Intuitively, we know it's in our best interest to stay on the front screen; it's where we want to live. Yet the side screen regularly steals our attention by introducing a perceived threat:

Kelly is a college sophomore who suffers from social anxiety. Walking across campus, she runs into a group of classmates. After exchanging a few awkward words, she heads off to class. As she leaves the interaction, her side screen lights up and she's hit with a jolt of insecurity. Her attention shifts from the external world—where she's walking, the surrounding sights and sounds—to the worries being displayed on the side screen in her mind. Scrolling across the side screen are thoughts of being a laughingstock. There are images of the group snickering behind her back. Similar to reviewing video footage, she studies the social interaction, frame by frame, analyzing facial expressions, scrutinizing what she said and how others reacted. She runs through her mind, over and over, an awkward pause that occurred in the brief exchange. Recalling a comment she made about the weather, she clenches her fists and says to herself, That was so stupid! Why did I say that? *As she focuses on the side screen, sorting through what she did or didn't say and how her peers may be responding, she becomes increasingly preoccupied and anxious.*

Kelly's experience demonstrates the power of the spotlight of attention. She can't control the anxiety or prevent its showing up. Her side screen was involuntarily activated as soon as she left the social interaction. Nor could she control the reflexive swivel of her internal eyes—her attention—when the fears announced themselves on the side screen. It's what she did next, once she found herself gazing at the brightly lit side screen, that got her into trouble. She kept the spotlight of attention on the worries and insecure feelings, which only increased their presence and strength.

The spotlight of attention perpetuates Kelly's social anxiety. Her habit of withdrawing from the here and now into her mind and analyzing the worries on the side screen, dissecting the details of her social experiences, only increases her insecurity and anxiety in her relationships. Though she doesn't realize it, the choices she makes with her mind—where she places her attention—energize the very worries and anxious feelings from which she seeks to free herself.

What we attend to gets energized. This internal reality can even be understood on a neurobiological level. According to Daniel Siegel, a leading expert in neurobiology, what you focus on in your mind—where you place your attention—gets translated into neuronal activity (PSYCHALIVE, n.d.). The process of attention actually directs and shapes neuronal firing in the brain, which becomes a problem when, as it is for Kelly, the object of attention is an unhelpful worry. As Kelly holds the spotlight of attention on the side screen, she unwittingly awakens and energizes a colony of neurons (nerve cells) in her brain that reinforce and give expression to her social anxiety.

Such attention functions like a heat lamp, warming and breathing life into your anxious thoughts and feelings. That's why redirecting attention to the front screen is a core principle of TSM. It's a simple concept with profound effects. When you take your attention off the side screen, as you'll learn to do in this book, you cut off one of its primary sources of energy. Without the benefit of your attention, the screen grows cold and gradually fades into the background.

The Second Source of Energy: Reactivity

Reactivity, the second source of energy, which often works in conjunction with the spotlight of attention, is the *Oh no!* reaction to the worries and anxious feelings showing up on the side screen: *That [insert fear here] can't happen!* or *I can't handle these feelings!* It's our resistance and fight against the experience of being under threat—feeling as if something of value in life is at risk. Here are a few examples:

SIDE SCREEN TRIGGER	PERCEIVED THREAT
Facing a confrontation	*This will end the friendship.*
Boarding the plane	*I'm going to panic and lose my mind!*
Reviewing an unfinished task	*I'll fail and disappoint everyone.*
Leaving a social interaction	*They think I'm stupid.*

When confronted with a threat, whether real or imagined, we react. We naturally resist and fight the alarming thoughts and feelings showing up on the side screen, which can show up in multiple forms. One common expression of reactivity is protesting and getting upset with the physiological experience of fear— how out of control or tense our body feels when we're anxious. Sitting around a conference table getting ready to speak, we get frustrated and ask ourselves: *Why am I so anxious right now? What's my problem? If I don't calm down, they'll hear a quiver in my voice and know I'm anxious.* Gripping the armrests just before takeoff, we internally exclaim, *I hate flying! I don't want to feel this way.*

Along with the anxious feelings, we also protest the thoughts—those anxious ideas that emotionally threaten what we care about in life. We don't want to accept or make space for the possibility of rejection or that some negative event could befall a loved one. These experiences, understandably, seem intolerable, so we react internally and operate on the perceived threat with our minds.

One common expression of this mental resistance and reactivity is *rumination*—a term also used to describe the process by which cows regurgitate and chew on previously consumed food. It's a good description of what we can do in our minds. We chew on and regurgitate worrisome thoughts, running them through our minds, over and over, as we desperately seek a way to dismantle the fear, such as reviewing all the reasons why someone won't break up with us or compulsively using WebMD to rule out a dreaded illness. We hold on to the belief that if we understand the fear well enough, if we get enough information and think through it the right way, the fear will somehow be resolved and we'll feel better—that WebMD will give us the relief we seek.

Alternatively, instead of chewing on the perceived concern, we may try to exert mental force on threatening thoughts, attempting to push them out of our mind. This form of reactivity is sometimes referred to as *undoing* thoughts, whereby you counter unsettling or anxious thoughts with positive ones. Plagued by thoughts of failure—going into a sales pitch or some important event—you attempt to neutralize the negative thoughts by repeatedly saying to yourself, *This will go well, this will go well…*This strategy holds the hope that the forceful presence of positive thoughts will negate the power of the threatening thoughts pushing into awareness.

However, just like the spotlight of attention, all these forms of reactivity only increase the prominence and volume of the anxious side screen. The more you try to fight anxious thoughts and feelings, the stronger they become.

The Third Source of Energy: Avoidance Behaviors

The third and final source of energy for the anxious side screen is avoidance behaviors. Anxiety is an aversive feeling that gives us the impression that we're under threat—that something important is at risk—and our natural, reflexive response is avoidance. When we know that something in life activates the anxious side screen, we instinctually try to avoid the identified trigger. We drive ten hours to a family event rather than risk the anxiety of flying. We stay in and watch a movie instead of risking rejection by asking someone out on a date. We take the stairs instead of the elevator (*not* for the exercise). We avoid taking healthy professional or personal risks for fear of failure. We avoid going to the doctor or dentist. We walk the other way to avoid the awkward social interaction. And the list goes on.

We avoid because we hold on to the hope that we can escape the anxious experience altogether, which makes sense. Who wants to feel anxious? This approach is understandable, but it backfires. Unknowingly, we are encouraging a conditioned fear response that brings more anxiety into our lives. The threat center, introduced at the opening of this chapter, is constantly scanning the environment for potential threats. When we act as if something is dangerous, which we do when we avoid something, our behavior confirms the validity of the perceived threat, and the threat center then catalogs it for our future protection. This sets the stage for increased anxiety, because any time we get close to or even contemplate the source of perceived danger, the brain will sound the alarm in the form of anxiety. The threat center thinks this helps us stay safe. And if we listen to the anxious alarm and continue the pattern of avoidance, we send yet another reinforcing message to the brain: *Thanks for warning me, brain…we need to stay away from that danger.* We end up reconfirming the validity of the threat. The next time the identified threat is detected, the brain screams even louder, and the cycle continues.

This happened to Jenny, a middle-aged woman I worked with who had a phobia of driving on freeways:

> *Jenny is at a stoplight. To the left is the freeway on-ramp—the fastest way to her destination. Straight ahead are surface streets. Just the thought of turning left elevates her anxiety, giving her a jolt of adrenaline. Fears of panicking and losing control of the car flood her mind. It's not worth it, she tells herself. Instead of turning left and getting on the freeway, she*

decides to take surface streets. There is instant relief. She relaxes her grip on the steering wheel and lets out a sigh. She feels safer and is thankful not to be on a freeway.

This natural avoidance of emotional danger comes at a cost. Jenny doesn't realize she's training her brain to be even more anxious about freeways. By avoiding the freeway, she sends a powerful message to her threat center: *Freeways are dangerous…something to be avoided… If I had turned left I would have been in danger.* Consequently, the next time Jenny gets close to an on-ramp, her brain, trying to keep her safe, will sound the anxious alarm even more loudly. This is exactly what happened. Her anxiety and fear response to freeways escalated, making it harder and harder for her to drive, even when she made a concerted effort to stay on surface streets. Soon even a reminder of the freeway, such as seeing an overpass or hearing a traffic report on the radio, could trigger a wave of panic.

Jenny's predicament demonstrates physical avoidance, the most common form, whereby we physically try to avoid known sources of fear. Sometimes, however, physical avoidance isn't possible. Either life demands that we not avoid the fear—say, we need to fly to an important business meeting—or the source of anxiety is harder to predict or control, such as the fear of failure or social judgment. When we must face these fears, despite our physical avoidance efforts, we may turn to a second form of avoidance: emotional avoidance. We try to escape the anxious experience on an emotional level. We try to run from the already activated side screen.

This was true for one of my patients, an executive named Vincent who was an anxious flyer. By the time he began treatment, he had a well-ingrained ritual of emotional avoidance when forced to fly. As soon as he boarded the aircraft, he popped two Xanax pills. Then he focused on getting to 10,000 feet, when the beverage cart would come down the aisle. At the first opportunity, he threw back a double Scotch, trying to block out the side screen and suppress his anxious thoughts and feelings.

Emotional avoidance also shows up in more subtle ways. A common example is avoiding conflict or backing down from a healthy confrontation. For some, even the idea of confronting another person makes them anxious—maybe they fear losing the relationship or fear they'll be verbally attacked or relationally punished in some way. When they detect tension in a relationship or see the potential for negative feelings, the anxious side screen is activated. To escape the anxious experience, these individuals do everything they can to free the relationship of the perceived tension and negative energy. They'll often agree with the other person and assume a submissive role instead of enduring the internal tension of voicing an alternative perspective.

Regardless of what form it takes, avoidance—physical or emotional—comes with a cost. Aside from strengthening the anxiety by creating a conditioned fear response, avoidance limits your personal freedom. The anxiety ends up defining the boundaries within which you can live. Your life sphere becomes constricted, you miss out on meaningful life events, and you end up compromising on values and goals that are important to you.

When Jenny, the woman with the freeway phobia, began treatment, she was distraught and overwhelmed by a sense of missing out—of not living the life she wanted. She hadn't seen two of her closest friends in a year because they lived on the other side of town, which required freeway travel. And she'd stopped attending her kids' away games. At first, her children protested and didn't understand her lack of attendance, but after a while they adjusted and stopped asking. The fact that her children had gotten used to her absence and no longer looked for her presence only compounded Jenny's sadness and sense of loss.

Now that we've identified how the anxious side screen is energized, the next step is learning to relate to your worries and anxious feelings in a new way that deprives them of these known sources of energy. In the next chapter, you'll learn the mental steps, as well as the emotional and behavioral reactions, that defuse anxious feelings and free the mind from worry.

Conclusion

This chapter represents part one of freeing yourself from the anxious side screen. You've become well acquainted with your personal side screen—the types of fears and worries that tend to show up in your life—and explored the three primary ways anxious thoughts and feelings are energized: through the *spotlight of attention*, resisting or fighting the anxious experience (*reactivity*), and *avoiding* sources of fear.

Now it's time for part two—relating to your anxious side screen in a new way that promotes mental and emotional freedom.

CHAPTER 3

FREEDOM FROM THE ANXIOUS SIDE SCREEN

An important step toward a life free of needless anxiety is becoming clear on the mental, emotional, and behavioral experiences that feed worries and anxious feelings, as explored in the previous chapter. We examined how watching side screen activity (spotlight of attention), fighting the experience (reactivity), and trying to avoid anxious feelings (avoidance behaviors) only empower the side screen and invite more anxiety into your life. There is power in recognizing these three energy sources—and you have now taken that first step.

Equipped with this information, in this chapter we move to helping you strike a new relationship with your anxious side screen that removes its power and influence from your life. When the worries come into your mind and you feel anxious, the key is responding in a way that deprives the side screen of needed energy. You want to develop a set of responses that doesn't collude with any of the three energy sources identified in the last chapter.

To accomplish this, we'll first work on correcting avoidance behaviors. As you read in chapter 2, if you repeatedly avoid a source of anxiety, you train the threat center to trigger the fear response in places where it doesn't belong—and you inadvertently teach yourself that anxiety is something you just can't handle. To recalibrate the system, you'll be introduced to the Freedom Ladder, the easiest and most efficient way of teaching your brain that something is not a threat worthy of the fear response. The Freedom Ladder will help you start correcting any avoidance behaviors you may have developed. Then you'll work on applying the principle of Accept & Redirect—accepting the presence of unwanted thoughts and feelings while redirecting your attention away from the side screen. This critical step of the Two-Screen Method protects you from watching the side screen (spotlight of attention) and purges your internal world of reactivity—the other two ways you can unwittingly energize the side screen. In the final section of the chapter, we'll take a deeper look at this concept of acceptance and the different ways you may be challenged in its application.

Correcting Avoidance Behaviors

Even though it feels unwise and unsafe, you need to move toward the fear. You need to expose yourself and stay present with the psychological threat from which you've been running. You can do this by developing a Freedom Ladder—called a *fear hierarchy* in exposure therapy—that will help you rate the things you fear in order of intensity, then devise a series of concrete, manageable tasks you can work through to systematically expose yourself to those things.

This requires courage. It's hard to let yourself feel anxious. In the beginning, it will feel as if you're betraying your protective instincts, knowingly putting yourself or something you value in jeopardy. But your courage will be rewarded. With each step forward, the fear will weaken. You'll notice that the dreaded event is not as bad as you thought. The longer you stay present with the fear, the less anxious you become. Soon you'll no longer feel the need to avoid the perceived threat, and you'll feel the satisfaction of expanding your personal freedom.

The easiest way to understand how exposure helps you achieve this is the train track analogy. If you bought a house near train tracks, it would be challenging for the first few days. The passing trains would register loudly, with the blasting horn, roaring, clanging, and vibration disrupting your sleep and distracting you throughout the day, and the threat center of your brain would consider them a potential threat. Similarly, anxiety, when you first begin to confront it, feels overwhelming. Yet if you stay in the house and remain exposed to the aversive stimuli—whether that's trains or your anxiety—your brain learns that the stimuli are not dangerous and it loses interest. After a few days you would take less notice and be less bothered by the passing trains, a sign that your brain has successfully acclimated to the noise; it works the same way with anxiety.

Climbing the Freedom Ladder is the equivalent of moving into the house near the tracks and purposefully exposing yourself to train noise. It's an opportunity to teach your brain that the things it finds unpleasant may be unpleasant, but they're not dangerous. At different points, especially in the beginning, your anxiety levels will be elevated. If you stay on task and don't fight the experience, your central nervous system will get used to the anxiety and turn down the volume. With each step you climb on the Freedom Ladder, you teach your central nervous system (the threat center) not to be afraid of the activity you once avoided—and you gain personal freedom.

BUILDING A FREEDOM LADDER

For a worksheet that will allow you to complete this exercise, visit http://www.newharbinger.com/42327.

To construct your own Freedom Ladder, ask yourself, "What activities am I avoiding because they make me anxious?" What activities would you like to participate in but don't because you associate them with anxiety? Make a comprehensive list of all the activities that come to mind, organized by anxious theme. If you suffer from social anxiety, for example, speaking up in a group, expressing your political views with a coworker, or asking for help at a store might show up on your list. If you suffer from chronic health fears, your list may include stepping inside a hospital, touching a public doorknob, or listening to a news report about the flu. Or, you may be afraid not of any given activity per se, but rather of the anxiety itself—you dread the anxious experience. In that case, the approach is the same: list the activities you avoid for fear of activating the anxiety and bringing on the anxious experience.

Once you have your list, go through it, rating the level of anxiety each activity generates on a scale of 0 to 100, with 0 representing no anxiety, 50 representing moderate anxiety, and 100 representing the highest level of anxiety. Ideally, you want to identify at least six or seven tasks at different anxiety levels, ranging from 40/100 to 100/100.

The socially anxious person, for example, might experience a 40/100 anxiety level asking a stranger for directions and a 100/100 anxiety level making a public announcement at church. This person would also want to identify social activities that generate anxiety at the 50/100, 60/100, 70/100, 80/100, and 90/100 levels. Her Freedom Ladder might look something like this:

100   Making an announcement at church

90   Walking into Home Depot and asking for the deli section

80   Skipping down the sidewalk when people are around

70   Offering a dissenting political view with someone you don't know well

60   Sending food back at a restaurant

50   Asking to try on an article of clothing at a retail store

40   Asking a stranger for directions

The pathway toward freedom starts with the 40/100 task or even a less anxious task, such as sitting down and constructing your Freedom Ladder or watching someone else engage in an embarrassing act on a YouTube video, which you might rate in the 20 to 30/100 range. Staying with our current Freedom Ladder example, our socially anxious person tackles the first rung of the ladder—asking a stranger for directions. Then a few days later, or the next week, she completes another 40/100 task or goes to the second rung on the ladder, the 50/100 activity (retail store). The week after that, she completes the 60/100 and 70/100 activities, upping the pace as she feels more confident about her capabilities. This continues until she has reached the top of the Freedom Ladder—the 100/100 task.

As you read this chapter, and the ones to follow, see if you can begin working your way up your Freedom Ladder. Begin with the activity or activities that you rated at 40/100 or lower. Then slowly begin ascending the rungs, applying and reinforcing the principles and strategies you're learning in this book. When you start out, the 100/100 task will seem unthinkable, but by the time you reach the dreaded activity, your relationship with anxiety will have changed. Along the way you'll build confidence in your ability to face fears. You'll notice the anxiety has less power than it used to and that you're not crushed by the feared activities. You'll discover that you can handle the anxiety and that the more you face it, the weaker it becomes. In fact, you may find the greatest challenge to be anticipatory anxiety, where it's not the activity itself that generates the most fear but rather thinking about it in advance. Once you engage in the activity, the actual experience may be anticlimactic; over time, this will decrease the anticipatory anxiety.

Addressing the Spotlight of Attention and Reactivity

Now that you have a structured way to correct avoidance behaviors (Freedom Ladder), let's turn to the other two sources of side screen energy: the *spotlight of attention* and *reactivity*—our automatic resistance to feeling under threat. These two anxious activators (attention and reactivity) often go hand in hand. You instinctually want to watch and monitor the incoming threats showing up on your side screen, while at the same time fighting their presence.

Consider Janet, a new teacher on the first day of class, wrestling with normal feelings of insecurity: *Will the students think I'm a good teacher? I hope I'm not too nervous.*

It comes time to deliver her lecture. It's going relatively well. Janet does spot some sleepy faces and quizzical looks in the classroom, but she tries not to be distracted. After a short break, the class reconvenes, and Janet realizes that a handful of students have not returned. Her underlying insecurity is activated. Negative thoughts rush in on her side screen:

The class is bored.
They think I'm a bad teacher.
What if no one shows up tomorrow?
I'm going to lose my job.

What is the normal reaction to this jolt of insecurity? How would we expect Janet to respond? Maybe the thoughts consume her attention, and she tries even harder to prove to others and herself that she's a good teacher. Maybe she seeks reassurance and engages some students near the lectern, hoping to elicit positive feedback about her teaching. Or maybe she mentally reviews the first part of the lecture, looking for evidence of where she "screwed up."

All of these common coping strategies carry unhelpful underlying assumptions, such as *I can't tolerate this feeling of insecurity* or *The class needs to like me.* If Janet attempts to get rid of the insecurity, she'll end up empowering the anxious side screen. Even if she finds a way to lower the anxiety in the moment, or for this particular class, it's only a matter of time before the fear returns. She'll continue to be stalked by a threat that requires ongoing vigilance and management, stealing her precious life energy and attention.

Instead of fighting or trying to push the insecurity away, Janet's pathway to freedom—and yours—is *emotional acceptance*. Ideally, she allows the insecurity to breathe on the side screen. She accepts the possibility that the students think she's a bad teacher. This doesn't mean she agrees or likes the idea of being a bad teacher. She just allows for the possibility on an emotional level. She allows it to be an unanswered question, reminding herself that she can live with her current emotional experience.

From there, Janet *redirects her attention*. In conjunction with letting go and softening her resistance around the anxious threat, Janet makes a concerted effort to focus her attention on the lecture notes and being present with the class, which in this context is the front screen. When her eyes wander back to the side screen, she gently redirects them back to her notes, the task at hand, and the present moment.

With her eyes on the front screen, Janet will still feel the presence of the side screen in her peripheral vision. It continues to kick off anxious energy. The insecure thoughts and feelings continue—*They're bored. They don't like the class.* This is distracting, and part of her mind may feel compromised. Through the noise, however, she stays focused on teaching. As she does, the feeling of insecurity slowly begins to lift, and she can evaluate the situation from a more balanced perspective. As time passes, she still spots some students with bored looks. But she also notices that a number of the students who seemed to have left when Janet resumed her lecture have trickled back into the classroom. And most students seem quite engaged with the lecture. Watching them nod and take notes as she's speaking makes it clear: most of them will come back tomorrow, and her job is not in jeopardy.

What Janet did to manage her performance anxiety and feelings of insecurity is the same thing you'll do for any threats that show up on your side screen: *accept* the presence of the challenging thoughts and feelings—to avoid the reactivity, the struggle or resistance, that breathes life into the anxiety—and *redirect* your attention from the side screen to the front screen, focusing on the parts of your life that matter. This act of Accept & Redirect, which is foundational to TSM, protects you from energizing the anxiety with your attention and reactivity. In subsequent chapters, you'll be introduced to the front screen anchors, which are designed to tether your attention and life energy to the front screen. As you'll see, having the alternative home for your mind that the front screen anchors offer is a helpful and important support in your application of Accept & Redirect. For the moment, however, we focus on your relationship to the side screen—the importance of applying emotional acceptance and rotating your attention away from the worries.

Part of applying Accept & Redirect is allowing the threats to go unattended in your peripheral vision. They're there, but you're careful not to make them the focus of your attention. This is hard to do. These threats on the anxious side screen will generate feelings of insecurity and plead for your attention. In these challenging spaces, it helps to say to yourself, *I can live with this feeling.* You remind yourself not to fight the experience of feeling under threat.

From there, you take a deep breath, encourage yourself to be patient, and when your attention wanders off to the threats on the side screen, keep gently redirecting it back to the front screen, such as the present moment. As you do this, sometimes repeatedly, you deprive the anxious side screen of energy and practice the art of redirection—the ability to focus and refocus at will on the object of your choosing, an important skill to have in your internal world. Exercising this skill will not only decrease the power and presence of anxiety in your life but also increase your capacity to enjoy the life-giving experiences playing out on your front screen.

What Exactly Am I Accepting?

In Janet's case, the process of accepting the threats being displayed on the side screen, while redirecting her attention to the front screen, went relatively smoothly. It's easy to relate to her experience, and we may be able to imagine applying acceptance to the same type of worries—about failure, being judged by others, and so on. But what about those fears that show up suggesting our very life is in danger? These types of fears can be more confusing and harder to accept.

Some people with a clean bill of health, for example, are visited by persistent health fears. For them, a lump in the throat can generate the thought, *Maybe I have throat cancer.* When the side screen lights up with this alarming idea, they actually feel as if the fear could be true and that their life is hanging in the balance, making acceptance and redirecting attention a harder task to accomplish.

Even though the threat status of throat cancer is higher than a fear of failure like Janet's, it's still a fear showing up on the side screen—a psychological threat generated by the mind. These individuals fearing cancer in the moment are confronted with the same choice as Janet's: do they dwell on the fear or redirect their attention to the front screen, taking the feeling of vulnerability with them?

While it's never easy, acceptance is easier to apply when the threat first shows up—and sometimes we're capable of practicing acceptance and redirecting our attention even with a grave thought like having cancer. When the anxious thought *Maybe I have throat cancer* first comes to mind, there's still distance between the person's core self and the fearful feeling; the person has yet to be sucked into the side screen, so applying the principle of acceptance at this stage can quickly defuse the fear. A few minutes or hours later, this person will often look back and wonder why he was so concerned about throat cancer.

The principle of acceptance is a powerful tool for defusing negative thoughts and feelings. It also takes a lot of courage to apply. For a brief period it will feel like you're accepting, on an emotional level, the reality of the threat. The professor on the first day of class will feel like a bad teacher ready to be fired; the client with health anxiety will feel the emotional reality of having throat cancer. By accepting the threat, you're not saying it's true or valid. On some level, you know the opposite to be true: that it's just a fear. Yet you try it on and allow the emotional reality of the threat to come in because you're the holder of important psychological wisdom: that while the fear *feels* real, it's actually something that lives inside you—a threat that is only psychological and will lose its power if you accept it.

The alternative to acceptance is trying to manage and fight off the endless stream of fears, insecurities, and anxieties generated by the side screen. As anxious people will often attest, they're dealing with "the worry of the moment." They're not concerned about the worry from last week; today there's another fear taking precedence. At some point, when the anxiety dissipates, they'll wonder why they were so preoccupied—*It seems silly that I was so afraid of having a brain tumor*—yet this repeated experience provides little comfort when the next anxious thought arrives. The feeling is hard to ignore. On some level, they know they shouldn't be so worried, but it feels real.

Even though the fear may be irrational and alarming and unwanted, accepting the feeling and the possibility of the threat is the quickest path to freedom. In the moment, as you accept the anxious story line produced by the side screen, it will feel as if you're risking something of value. Yet you choose the path of acceptance and nonresistance because you know this internal stance will deprive the side screen of needed energy and set you free from an anxious life.

The Three Layers of Acceptance

In this chapter, the focus has been on changing your relationship with the side screen so you can be free of anxiety and live a full life. As we've highlighted, this relationship, which is captured in the Accept & Redirect directive, should be defined by acceptance—which is one of the most powerful antidotes to anxious thoughts and feelings. After the side screen is activated, however, your willingness to accept the unwanted internal experience will be tested in a variety of ways. To keep your relationship with the side screen free of resistance and to ensure that you're not giving it energy, you need to be aware of the three layers of acceptance:

- Accepting the specific threat being displayed on the side screen

- Accepting the experience of anxiety—the intense, deeply uncomfortable feelings it can create

- Accepting the pull of the side screen and the need to redirect your internal eyes to the front screen, over and over again

To demonstrate, let's return to Jenny, the woman in the previous chapter who suffers from anxiety about driving—especially when freeways are involved.

The First Layer: Accepting the Threat

As we get into the car, Jenny says, "What if I lose control?" She is speaking to her core fear of losing control while driving— the specific threat being displayed on her side screen. In today's session, we're continuing with the exposure therapy, which means Jenny is going to do the very thing she's afraid to do. Drive! She imagines panicking, losing control of her rational mind, and letting go of the steering wheel. Her fear, as you'll recall, is heightened when driving on freeways—the place we're headed for today's exposure therapy session. For Jenny, freeways are especially activating because cars are going faster, split decisions need to be made, and the consequences of losing control are greater than on surface streets.

Scrolling across Jenny's side screen is, *While driving on the freeway I'm going to lose control and crash the car.* This fear causes her to police her physiological responses. From an internal watchtower, she watches her bodily symptoms with an air of suspense.

She studies the physical sensations taking place in her body for any evidence that she's losing control.

"I know it's hard," I tell her, "but you need to allow for the possibility...allow the anxious idea of losing control to be there... Don't fight it...allow the fear to be there on the side screen, but don't watch it. Take your attention off your body and place it on the road—the front screen."

To break free from the anxiety, Jenny needs to stop fighting the idea of losing control. The idea of losing control is unthinkable to Jenny. In her mind, this is something she can't accept. To lose control means a car accident. How could she accept that? Yet by moving into acceptance she's *not* accepting or agreeing to a car accident. She's creating space for the possibility. She's allowing herself to feel the danger. She's taking the psychological or emotional risk that she could lose control. The operative term here is *emotional risk*. Internally she feels out of control, but in reality she's able to drive.

I am seated next to her. I can see that she's in control of the vehicle. In fact, she's being a cautious and vigilant driver—maybe one of the safest drivers on the freeway. There is her emotional reality and then there is objective reality. For her to get in touch with a more balanced perspective and see the situation more objectively, the anxiety needs to subside. Only then will she see the situation with a fresh pair of eyes.

As we approach the on-ramp, Jenny feels a flood of anxiety. She's lightheaded and nauseated, and her heart pounds. She grips the steering wheel and says, "I don't think I can do this!" Every fiber of her being screams *Danger!* She feels totally out of control. She doesn't believe she can drive in her current state.

The Second Layer: Accepting the Experience of Anxiety

Even when your eyes are firmly planted on the front screen, you may still feel the physiological impact of anxiety and have the experience of being heckled from the sidelines. Jenny, gripping the steering wheel and moving ever closer to the on-ramp, is now being tested on a second level. She needs to accept what's happening in her body—the intense physiological experience of fear. "Just allow your body to feel what it needs to feel," I tell her. "Don't fight the anxiety…let go and allow yourself to ride the wave of anxiety."

In the moment, I understand the challenge of following my direction. Jenny has been avoiding freeways for years. This avoidance has taught her brain to send a fear signal in the proximity of a freeway. Now she isn't just close to a freeway, but actually getting on one! Her brain, in an effort to keep her safe, is sounding the loudest alarm it can, and her body's responding as if she were in extreme danger. But, as she accepts the anxious physiology as it spikes, she experiences a shift. The spike slowly subsides over the course of a few minutes.

In Jenny's case, her anxiety is highly physiological, so the second layer of acceptance will be primarily focused on her uncomfortable physical sensations. In other cases, such as with obsessive anxiety, accepting the experience of anxiety is more about accepting being heckled or taunted from the sidelines. You continue socializing, for example, even when the side screen is shouting out negative, insecure messages in response to a comment you made: "That was a dumb thing to say," "People find you boring," and so on. This is obviously distracting and makes socializing more difficult. But you accept the distracting influence, redirecting your attention to the conversation in the present moment as it plays out on your front screen.

The Third Layer: Accepting the Need to Keep Accepting

The third layer is accepting the side screen's pull and the repeated need to redirect your eyes to the front screen. To accept and redirect isn't a one-and-done process; you might need to do it any number of times to train your internal eyes to look where you want them to.

As Jenny faces her fear, her brain is quickly learning that driving on freeways is not an alarming threat, and her anxiety drops significantly. Yet she still feels a pull from the side screen. She feels okay now, but she fears this could change at any moment; there is still the threat of loss of control. She tries to keep her eyes on the front screen, but they keep wandering to physical sensations, looking for signs she's losing control. She grows frustrated because she doesn't want to watch the side screen. She doesn't want to empower the anxiety, so she continually redirects her eyes back to the front screen. Finally, she asks, "Why can't I just focus on driving?"

"Don't get angry or frustrated with yourself if your eyes keep going to the side screen," I tell her. "Sometimes the pull of the side screen is so strong your eyes will repeatedly dart over to it despite your best efforts. Your job is to keep redirecting back to the front screen." Jenny follows this advice, and while it's clear some traces of the discomfort linger, in the end she does manage to focus on driving.

When you first start applying acceptance to anxiety, you will do a lot of redirecting. You're building a new muscle set: the ability to train your internal eyes in the direction you want. Gently and nonjudgmentally, just keep redirecting your eyes back to the front screen. You want to resist beating yourself up for having to continually redirect, because this frustration will translate into energy—something we don't want to give the side screen.

Conclusion

In this chapter, we explored how to relate to your side screen in a new way. We started with the Freedom Ladder, a systematic way of correcting avoidance behaviors. As you gradually approach your fear, you teach your threat center that certain experiences, such as feeling embarrassed or failing, are unpleasant, but they're not a danger to you or deserving of the fear response.

After showing you a way of recalibrating your fear response—and turning down the volume on your anxious side screen—with the Freedom Ladder, we focused on the principle of Accept & Redirect: accepting the anxious thoughts and feelings showing up on your side screen, while redirecting your attention to the front screen. By following the Accept & Redirect directive, you protect yourself from energizing the side screen with your attention (spotlight) and reactivity. In the final section, we took a deeper look at what acceptance is and the three ways you may need to apply it as you break free from the pattern of anxious worry.

In the next chapter, you'll be introduced to the first front screen anchor—Mindfulness Skills—which will help you stay tethered to the front screen as you're redirecting attention away from the side screen (applying Accept & Redirect).

CHAPTER 4

MINDFULNESS SKILLS ANCHOR
Tethering Your Mind to the Present Moment

A primary theme in the Two-Screen Method is mindfulness. The image of the two screens helps you find the internal space between suppression—pushing unwanted thoughts and feelings out of awareness—and preoccupation, the act of dwelling and ruminating on anxious concerns or sources of pain. When you bring the image of two screens to mind, you naturally create space between your core self—as the person observing—and the surrounding thoughts and feelings. You can see and feel the activity showing up on the side screen without being consumed by or overidentifying with the content being generated. By recalling a simple visual, you'll be in an ideal position to strike the balance between suppression and preoccupation that is a primary goal of mindfulness.

In TSM, mindfulness is also applied in how you relate to the side screen—specifically, with acceptance. You accept, rather than fight, the worries coming into your mind. You are encouraged to give space to the painful or insecure feeling, while not focusing your attention on this side screen content. When the side screen lights up, you accept the presence of the challenging thoughts and feelings, while redirecting your attention to the front screen.

This chapter expands on your application of mindfulness by helping you cultivate present-moment awareness with the Mindfulness Skills anchor. This front screen anchor is a powerful ally in helping you find and stay tethered to the present moment, when the side screen is vying for your attention. Having a reliable way of entering the present moment will protect your mind from investing in the side screen content, an act that only intensifies the worries or anxious feelings. In addition to this protective factor, developing mindfulness skills—the ability to be in the present moment—has the added benefit of promoting relaxation and positive mood states (Hoffman, Sawyer, Witt, & Oh, 2010).

What Is Mindfulness?

You may have questions about this term *mindfulness*—what it means, how to define it, where it comes from, and how it can help you. It was described only briefly in chapter 1, and it can be a hard concept to wrap your head around. In fact, even in the field of psychology there is no agreed-upon definition of mindfulness. One that's frequently cited comes from Jon Kabat-Zinn, a pioneer in the mindfulness movement of psychology. In his book *Wherever You Go, There You Are* (1994), he defines mindfulness as "paying attention in a particular way; on purpose, in the present moment, and nonjudgmentally" (p. 4). Others in the field have felt the need to define mindfulness more narrowly, stressing the person's relationship to internal sensations. Here's how Carson and his colleagues defined mindfulness in a 2004 article in *Behavior Therapy*:

> [Mindfulness] is a perspective on thoughts and feelings that cultivates recognition of them as passing events in the mind rather than identifying with them or treating them as necessary reflections of reality. (Carson, Carson, Gil, & Baucom, 2004, p. 472)

While there is no uniform definition of mindfulness in the psychological literature, the most widely used and accepted definitions contain three primary themes:

- Observing inner experience as an impartial spectator, where you don't layer meaning or judgments or automatically identify with the thoughts and feelings coming into awareness

- Accepting—not resisting or fighting—painful or unwanted thoughts and feelings

- Attending to the present moment

The Emergence of Mindfulness in Psychology

Kabat-Zinn introduced mindfulness into the field of psychology in the late 1970s, while working at the Massachusetts Medical Center as a medical professor. From an early age, Kabat-Zinn had a penchant for thinking outside the box and seeing natural partnerships across disciplines. Influenced by an artistic mother and a data-driven, scientific father, he cultivated a curiosity about how people perceived reality and the nature of consciousness. Eventually these interests took him to MIT, where he pursued studies in molecular biology and attended lectures on an array of topics, including Zen Buddhism and other Eastern perspectives being offered in the 1960s.

Years later, at the Massachusetts Medical Center, while trying to develop a treatment approach that would bring relief to chronic pain patients, he noticed that these patients tended to react in ways that only made the pain worse. People with lower-back pain, for example, might dwell on the pain or become angry and frustrated with their condition—*Why is this happening to me? Will this pain ever stop?! I can't live with this pain!* These types of reactions, he hypothesized, inflamed negative feeling states and increased stress levels, which only exacerbated the pain and intensified suffering. Kabat-Zinn wondered if he could help this group by reshaping their relationship—their pattern of responses—to the pain through the practice of mindfulness.

He went to work and developed an eight-week program to teach the core principles of mindfulness. In 1979, at the hospital's Stress Reduction Clinic, the first class of mindfulness-based stress reduction (MBSR) was offered. The original participants practiced breath meditation, engaged in light yoga, participated in body awareness exercises, and learned techniques that helped them experience thoughts, feelings, and physical sensations with curiosity, presence of mind, and acceptance. After eight weeks of MBSR, most of these original participants reported a significant reduction in pain. The mindfulness training lowered their stress levels and helped them strike a healthy relationship with the pain. By accepting and not fighting the pain, many group members experienced an increased sense of well-being and were able to return to a more active lifestyle (Kabat-Zinn, 1990).

Others in the field, taking note of MBSR's successes—and making their own discoveries—started treating other symptoms and conditions with this mindfulness approach. Consistently, mindfulness was found to be effective in alleviating emotional and psychological distress. It wasn't long before mindfulness-based therapies began to emerge, such as acceptance and commitment therapy (ACT), mindfulness-based cognitive therapy (MBCT), and dialectical behavior therapy (DBT). Today these therapies are considered evidence-based treatments and are helping thousands of people overcome debilitating psychological symptoms and behaviors (Hayes, Luoma, Bond, Masuda, & Lillis, 2006; Juarisco, Forman, & Herbert, 2010; Ost, 2008; Twohig et al., 2010; Hoffman, et al., 2010; Kleim, Kröger, & Kosfelder, 2010).

Each year, the proven effectiveness of mindfulness increases its presence in the field of psychology. Currently, mindfulness-based treatments are being used to successfully treat depression, anxiety, borderline personality disorder, cancer side effects, anger problems, eating disorders, and sexual dysfunction, to name a few (Althof, 2010; Kabat-Zinn et al., 1992; Kristeller & Hallett, 1999; Linehan, 1993; Segal, Williams, & Teasdale, 2002; Speca, Carlson, Goodey, & Angen, 2000).

Mindfulness in the Two-Screen Method

Like other mindfulness-based approaches, the Two-Screen Method places a strong emphasis on present-moment aware-ness—developing your ability to fully experience life as it's hap-pening right now, in this moment. This important ability is cultivated with the Mindfulness Skills anchor, the subject of this chapter.

The Mindfulness Skills anchor has two primary features or areas of focus. The first is general mindfulness training through the regular practice of breath meditation and engaging in routine activities with the intention of applying mindfulness principles. These practices are good stress reducers and will increase your capacity to focus attention on the object of your choosing. This is an important skill to have when the side screen is activated and you want to stay connected to the front screen. With time, you will find it easier to keep your awareness in the present moment, or on the task at hand, when the side screen is generating dis-tracting thoughts and feelings.

The second feature of the Mindfulness Skills anchor is pro-viding help in the midst of challenging moments. At times you may feel emotionally overwhelmed or flooded or stuck in an endless loop of worries. You may find it difficult—if not impossi-ble—to shift your focus to the front screen and relate to the chal-lenging thoughts and feelings showing up on the side screen in a way that will dissipate them. The Mindfulness Skills anchor equips you with a powerful strategy that quickly and effectively brings your mind into the present moment, so you can take a step back, regroup, and reengage the challenging thoughts and feel-ings with increased psychological freedom and flexibility.

General Mindfulness Training

By the time we reach adulthood, we've adopted thousands of cognitive templates for daily living. We get behind the wheel and upload the "drive car" template. We're driving, but we're not really there. We may even wonder, coming out of a dreamlike state, *Who's been driving for the last ten miles?* This same phenomenon of life on autopilot takes place in front of the kitchen sink, folding the laundry, taking a shower, talking with others, and countless other activities. Our body is there going through the motions, but our mind is somewhere else.

This tendency to mentally check out happens because we assume the activity is fully known. It registers as old and familiar, offering nothing new to experience. The task before us is simply a life obligation that doesn't require our full attention. In an attempt to either escape the perceived boredom or maximize efficiency, our thoughts and attention travel to other subject matters—the next item on the to-do list, an idea for an upcoming project, a recent conversation, and so on.

Mindfulness training disrupts this pattern of living life on autopilot. With time, it helps you recapture some of the awestruck sensibilities lost in the early years of life. These sensibilities are a major reason why young children experience so much joy and make us smile when we watch them play. Free of cognitive templates, they experience the world as a sensory playground, with stimulating discoveries and hidden treasures around every corner. They will stop in their tracks and stare with amazement at a wet leaf reflecting sunlight. Running into the neighbor's dog triggers a joy-filled giggle. Their open, unbiased minds free them up to fully capture the miraculous all around them.

To free yourself from stale cognitive templates and experience the other benefits of mindfulness, you need to do some mindfulness training. TSM's practical, streamlined approach provides two categories of exercises that you can easily incorporate into your busy life. First, you will get familiar with the foundational breath meditation—the act of focusing solely on your breathing.

Next, you'll work on infusing your ordinary activities of life—those things that often feel like a pain or burden—with more color and stimulation by approaching them with mindful awareness.

THE BREATH MEDITATION

With this meditation you enter a quiet space with the intention of focusing only on your breath—the air coming in and the air going out. Before introducing you to a version of the breath meditation called focused breathing awareness (FBA), it's important to examine how you breathe.

The breath. Breathing is something most of us do with little thought—it just happens. Approximately twenty thousand times per day, we inhale life-sustaining oxygen and exhale carbon dioxide. It's an automatic or *autonomic* process—that is, it happens without conscious effort—so we are generally unaware of exactly how we're accomplishing it. Unknowingly, we may be engaging in thoracic or chest breathing, which tends to be more shallow and less rhythmic and is associated with a host of negative physiological symptoms, including muscle tension, irregular heart rates, and anxiousness.

Ideally, you want to train yourself to breathe from your diaphragm, a parachute-shaped sheet of muscle between the lower lungs and the organs in the abdominal cavity. When you breathe diaphragmatically, you will notice your belly rising and falling with each inhale and exhale. This diaphragmatic breathing is deeper and more rhythmic than chest breathing. It achieves the ideal balance of oxygen and carbon dioxide in your body and is associated with lower stress and increased relaxation.

You can readily determine whether your breathing is diaphragmatic by placing a hand on your abdomen. As you inhale, you should notice your hand rising. As you exhale, you should notice your hand going down. You may also find it helpful to visualize a balloon in your abdomen. On the inhale, you fill the balloon up with air, as your abdomen rises. On the exhale, the air is released from the balloon and your abdomen drops accordingly.

Once you get the idea of diaphragmatic breathing and have practiced it a few times, you're ready for the breath meditation, focused breathing awareness (FBA), described next. Over the next eight weeks, try to carve out ten to fifteen minutes each day (or several times per week) to practice this exercise. If you commit to this schedule, you'll feel less stressed and notice being more present with the people and life activities on your front screen.

FOCUSED BREATHING AWARENESS (FBA)

This exercise is about observing and following your breath. Your only job for the next few minutes is to notice the air coming in and the air going out. Everything else in life can wait.

Begin by finding a comfortable place to sit down with as few distractions as possible. After you've assumed a relaxed but attentive posture, close your eyes and take a deep breath. As you exhale, allow yourself to let go and release any tension present in your body. Take a second deep breath and on the exhale, remember to relax as you release the air.

After your second deep breath, allow your breathing to flow freely and naturally. Now turn your attention to it. Follow the air coming in and the air going out. Don't be surprised if your mind wanders. This is to be expected. Just keep gently redirecting your attention back to the breath.

One effective way to anchor your attention to the breath, especially in the beginning, is to count each breath on the exhale. You take in a breath and then on the first exhale you say to yourself *one*. Then after taking in the second breath, on the exhale you count *two*. Repeat this pattern for the third and fourth breaths. After counting four exhales, start back at one again, counting another four breaths. Repeat this cycle for ten to fifteen minutes.

Understanding your experience of FBA. What was your experience of this exercise? Were there times when your attention drifted? That's perfectly natural. The mind loves to wander—to to-do lists, random thoughts, images from a recent social interaction, questions about why you're following your breath, and so on. An endless stream of thoughts and feelings will compete with your goal of watching and following the breath. This can be frustrating. But it's entirely normal. The key is to stay patient and committed to redirecting your attention back to the breath.

This repeated redirection of attention is an important part of mindfulness training. It simulates real life and how you want to respond. In the middle of a conversation (front screen), your mind can take off with a worry (side screen). You can be in the car listening to a news story when your mind, triggered by something you've heard, starts to review all the times you've felt mistreated by others. In these situations, your sense of well-being—the state of your internal world—will be determined by what you do with the spotlight of your attention. Ideally, you want to redirect the spotlight back to the present moment on the front screen. The FBA exercise gives you a safe place to practice and strengthen this discipline of redirection. As your mind wanders, you keep bringing it back to the breath—over and over again.

If you felt overstimulated or overwhelmed by internal activity—racing thoughts or intense feelings—when you closed your eyes to follow the breath, there's an easy adjustment you can make to change your experience. Instead of closing your eyes, find a visual anchor in your environment—maybe a spot on the wall or floor. The visual anchor shouldn't be too stimulating or distracting; rather, look for a neutral place to rest your eyes as you attend to the breath. Once you have the visual anchor in place, proceed with the FBA exercise.

SPIRITUAL INTEGRATION

If you're looking for an opportunity to integrate your spiritual life into your mindfulness training, the breath meditation offers a natural platform. The practice of following your breath, which you just experienced, can also be a time to open up your awareness and attune to that which goes beyond self. In fact, the meditative practice of attuning to the presence of God (or however you conceptualize your higher power) is an ancient spiritual practice widely forgotten. As you practice the following exercise, use the spiritual framework that's most comfortable for you.

ATTUNING TO THE PRESENCE OF GOD

Find a comfortable and quiet place where you can sit down and take a break from the busyness of the day.

Once you get settled in, take a few deep or medium-sized breaths, allowing yourself to let go and release any built-up tension.

Allow your breathing to flow naturally without trying to change it in any way. Take a moment to reflect on this gift—this breath of life that is always with you. This breath you're watching is one marker of a greater presence in your life.

As you begin following your breath, imagine—with each inhale—that you're drawing in God's loving and peaceful presence, something that is all around you in this very moment. With each exhale, try to release the worries and concerns of this world. Right now you're allowing yourself to be still and cared for in that presence. Feel the peace and comfort as you let go.

Begin using the counting method to help you follow the breath. With each inhale, imagine soaking in God's presence. Following the first breath, say *one* to yourself as you exhale. Take in a second breath—and with it God's presence—and say *two* on the second exhale. After counting four breaths in this manner, start the counting back at one again, repeating this pattern for ten to fifteen minutes, allowing yourself to richly experience God's presence during this sacred yet simple act of breathing.

DAILY ACTIVITIES WITH MINDFULNESS

In addition to the breath meditation, TSM has you develop mindfulness by engaging in routine activities with the goal of present-moment awareness. Instead of going elsewhere in your mind, you awaken the senses and approach any task—whether it's washing the dishes, brushing your teeth, or sorting through the mail—as a curious detective would. You notice the tactile sensations—how the object feels in your hand. You breathe in and study the aroma of the toothpaste or dishwashing soap. You look for different textures and shades of light on the envelope or plate you're holding. You listen to the sounds of the running water or the car engine or the envelope as you open it. You intentionally attune with and immerse yourself in the experience using the five senses. This mindful approach can inject unexpected aliveness and pleasure into your life, even in the midst of routine activities.

Here are two examples of approaching a routine task with mindfulness. The goal is to designate at least a couple of occasions per week where you implement the mindfulness approach to a life activity for ten to fifteen minutes.

WASHING DISHES WITH MINDFULNESS

As you approach the dishes, make the commitment to stay fully present. Remind yourself that you are not going to *do* the dishes but rather *experience* the dishes. Feel the warm soapy water. Notice your body movements as you wash each dish. Slow down and fully enter the experience. What do you see? What is the color, shape, and texture of each item you're handling? Notice how the light dances off each object. Slow down and take your time with each one. When your mind wanders, gently and nonjudgmentally bring it back to the most noticeable sensation, such as the water temperature. Using all of your senses, stay curious and present with the experience for ten to fifteen minutes.

MINDFUL DRIVING

As you approach the car, notice how it looks. What color is it? How would you describe its shape? Make note of how the handle feels as you open the driver's side door.

As you take a seat, remind yourself to be curious and fully present with the act of driving. Feel your hands wrapped around the steering wheel. Take a look around the interior. What do you see? Notice how your body feels in the seat. Pay attention to the sounds of the engine as it starts up.

As you begin driving, notice the road ahead—the texture, the color, the lane dividers and other traffic markings on the road. Open up your scope of awareness, taking in the experience of driving with all its sights, sounds, and tactile experiences. (Of course, don't get so absorbed in your surroundings that you lose safe control.) Stay aware and fully present with the act of driving. When your mind wanders, use one of the five senses to bring yourself back into the driving experience. Maintain this mindful intention and disposition for ten to fifteen minutes.

There is nothing sacrosanct about these two mindfulness examples. You can apply the same principles—committing yourself to being present as you begin an activity, noticing the movements you make and the impressions you get as you complete the activity, and bringing your mind back to the present moment any time it wanders as you complete the activity—to any routine activity. And you're encouraged to experiment. Which activities will you bring mindful presence to in the next few weeks? Jot down a list and commit yourself to the practice.

As we conclude this section on general mindfulness training, note that the material presented in this chapter is not intended to be a comprehensive mindfulness program. The recommended exercises are designed only to give you the base required to apply the Two-Screen Method and make the desired change in your life. If you want to go further with mindfulness, there are many great resources, such as A *Mindfulness-Based Stress Reduction Workbook* (Stahl & Goldstein, 2010) or Jon Kabat-Zinn's classic book *Full Catastrophe Living* (2013). There are also a host of helpful apps, such as Headspace and Calm, for practitioners at any level that guide you through the steps and practice of mindfulness. You're encouraged to take advantage of these aids and develop deeper roots in your understanding and experience of mindfulness.

Mindfulness Skills for Challenging Moments

Up to this point, the focus has been on general mindfulness training through the regular practice of FBA and approaching tasks of everyday life with mindful intention. This feature of the Mindfulness Skills anchor makes it easier to stay in and return to the present moment; it also has the benefit of promoting relaxation and infusing life with more color and aliveness (Langer & Moldoveanu, 2000).

Much of the time—especially after practicing the exercises outlined in this chapter—applying the Mindfulness Skills anchor is a straightforward process. After catching yourself on the side screen (*I'm starting to worry right now*), you gently remind yourself to redirect attention to the front screen, which in the context of the current chapter is the present moment—staying focused on the current conversation, the words you're reading on this page, the landscape around you, and so on.

Applying this first step of TSM—accepting the thoughts and feelings on the side screen and redirecting to the front screen—becomes more challenging, however, when the worries and painful feelings are more intense. On occasion, you may feel emotionally flooded or hopelessly tangled up in anxious worries, and—despite your best efforts—unable to apply the Accept & Redirect directive. This can certainly happen in the midst of a panic attack or an all-consuming craving. The second feature of the Mindfulness Skills anchor can help you at these times.

In this next section, you will learn a powerful technique known as grounding, a fast, reliable way to anchor your mind to the present moment, allowing you to get some healthy space from the internal storm.

GROUNDING SKILLS

Grounding is a systematic method of anchoring your attention and person to the present moment. Think of it as mindfulness on steroids, where the goal of present-moment awareness is carried out with intense focus. Here's how it works. Wherever you find yourself, you hyperfocus on your surroundings using the five senses. You listen intently to all the sounds you can detect in the room or current environment. You study the color and texture of the walls. You notice your body's pressure on the chair and the sensation of your feet against the floor. If food is involved or you have a breath mint (or the like) available, you closely inspect these items for smell and taste. You rally all of your senses to decisively lean into the present moment.

What makes grounding so valuable—and a lifeline at critical times—is the way it changes how your brain is functioning. When you're emotionally flooded or can't stop worrying, you're stuck in a particular region of the brain known as the *narrative focus* network (Farb et al., 2007). This network of neurons in the brain lights up when your attention goes internal—when your mind leaves the present moment to contemplate ideas, images, memories, and emotional experiences in your internal world. There is nothing inherently wrong with this narrative focus. In fact, you need to do this to solve problems, to remember your wedding day, to plan for retirement, even to experience personal growth, which requires self-reflection. Without mental reflection (narrative focus) it would be hard to make sense of life experiences and form a coherent self-identity. This type of mental activity just needs to be exercised with caution, for it's in the narrative focus that worrying and investing in destructive moods takes place. It's the place in your brain where you can get stuck and overwhelmed by the side screen.

Grounding—this act of sensory hyperfocus—helps because it automatically pops you out of the narrative focus and ushers you into a completely different region of the brain known as the *experiential focus* network (Farb et al., 2007). The experiential focus network is activated when your attention and awareness are tied to the present moment—your experience of self in the here and now. And what's most interesting—and helpful—is that you can't be in both brain networks at the same time. You're in either the narrative focus or the experiential focus. The two systems are neurologically incompatible. That means if you have a reliable way of activating the experiential focus—such as the act of grounding—you also have a reliable way to pop out of the narrative focus and free yourself from the overwhelming side screen activity.

Here is a grounding exercise you can begin practicing and using for those times when you feel consumed and overwhelmed by the side screen.

GROUNDING EXERCISE

Begin by taking a deep breath and holding it, noticing the tension it creates in your body. After three to five seconds, slowly release the air, telling yourself to let go and relax. Repeat this sequence a second time.

Wherever you find yourself, begin hyperfocusing on your surroundings with all your senses—starting with the auditory sense. Listen intently to all the sounds you can detect in your immediate environment. For the moment, allow this to be your only job—everything else can wait.

After hyperfocusing on sound, find a visual anchor in the environment and study it. Examine its color, texture, and pattern. Notice every detail so that you could describe it to someone or draw the object from memory later.

After about one minute, shift from the visual to the tactile sensory experience. Move your hand across the nearest table or desk, noticing the temperature and pressure against your palm. Feel the fabric or material of your chair. Take note of how your body feels—your hands resting on your lap, the pressure of your feet against the ground, and so on.

After thirty to sixty seconds, shift to the olfactory sense. Take in a deep breath and either study the aroma of the room or go grab a tea bag or spice or something else with a pleasing scent. Like a detective, analyze the smell for approximately sixty seconds.

Once you've completed this grounding sequence, you should feel more anchored and less overwhelmed. That doesn't mean the anxious thoughts and feelings are gone. The narrative focus network—the place where you've been caught up in the worries or anxious experience—is still cooling down and could easily be reignited. To protect your mind from getting sucked back in, try to engage for at least a few minutes in an activity that naturally places your attention in the external world, such as conversing with a friend or coworker, helping the kids with homework, or picking up household supplies at the store.

You're encouraged to regularly practice and implement, as needed, these grounding techniques. At the same time, you may find yourself in situations—because of time pressures, lack of privacy, or some other limitation—where it's not possible to take this comprehensive approach to grounding. Perhaps you're hit with an anxious spike a few minutes before your presentation, or your mind is stuck on an anxious thought when a loved one needs your full attention, or you're in the middle of an exam and you're so anxious you can't think straight.

Fortunately, you can modify and streamline the grounding technique for these real-life situations, without sacrificing much benefit. This shortcut will still activate the experiential focus, popping you out of the narrative focus, where you've gotten stuck in the overwhelming thoughts and feelings, and anchoring you in the present moment.

MORE WAYS TO PRACTICE GROUNDING

The first step in creating a streamlined version of grounding is determining which of the five senses offers the best hook for your attention. As you practice the standard grounding exercise introduced earlier, take mental notes. Which sensory experience fully captures your attention, making your mind less likely to wander? Maybe there are two sensory experiences that stand out, such as focusing on a sound and visually studying an object or aspect of your immediate surroundings. The idea is to explore your sensory experience so you can identify the top one or two best holders of your attention.

Once you've identified these, you're ready for the abbreviated version. Instead of taking a tour of all five senses, when circum-stances don't allow for the full protocol, go to and stay with the top sense or senses you've identified: hyperfocus only on the sounds you can hear, or hyperfocus solely on the tactile sensory experience—whatever is your most effective tether to the exter-nal world.

When applying this abridged version of grounding, consider too the particular context in which you find yourself. Ideally, you want to hyperfocus on those aspects of the environment that support your values and the purpose or goal of the activity. If important information is being shared, for example, you may want to hyperfocus on each word being uttered by the speaker (sound). If you're swimming laps in a pool, and the worry machine is up and running, you may want to attune to how your body feels (tactile) moving through the water. If you're frantically scurrying around the house getting ready for guests to arrive, it could be the visual sense that best supports your immediate goals.

You may need only two minutes—a mere 120 seconds—of hyperfocusing to pop out of the narrative focus and enter the present moment. After you've applied the grounding for a couple of minutes, try to implement the first step of the Two-Screen Method (Accept & Redirect). Accept the anxious thoughts and feelings showing up on the side screen, while rotating your internal eyes to the present moment on the front screen. If you still feel overwhelmed by the side screen activity and are unable to apply this step, you may need to do another round of hyperfocusing. Take another minute or two where you give your full attention and life energy to one or more of your senses.

Conclusion

In this chapter, you were introduced to the first of the three front screen anchors: Mindfulness Skills, designed to increase your capacity for present-moment awareness in both your everyday life (mindfulness training) and challenging emotional spaces (grounding techniques).

The first part of the chapter focused on general mindfulness training through the practice of watching your breath (focused breathing awareness) and engaging the normal tasks of life with the full intention of being present—using your five senses to fully experience the act of driving or washing dishes or whatever the task might be. Through these practices you increase your capacity for present-moment awareness, lower your stress, and add some needed stimulation and interest to the routine tasks of life.

The second part of the chapter focused on using the Mindfulness Skills anchor for challenging moments. You learned how to use grounding—hyperattuning to your immediate environment using all five senses—when you're emotionally flooded or stuck on looping negative thoughts. We also explored how you can modify and streamline the grounding technique to fit the real-life circumstances and challenges you face.

Up to this point, the focus has been on breaking free of worries and anxious feelings, a mission that we'll continue throughout the book. Beginning with the next chapter, you'll have the opportunity to expand your application of the Two-Screen Method to other challenges showing up in your internal world. As it turns out, the same principle that defuses anxious thoughts and feelings (Accept & Redirect) can be used to free you from depressed moods or the side screen activity that fuels destructive habits. It's common to struggle with more than just one issue, so having a universal approach to decrease the power and presence of side screen activity, regardless of what it is—anxiety, negative moods, unhealthy cravings, and so on—is incredibly helpful.

CHAPTER 5

THE ADDICTIVE SIDE SCREEN
The Island of the Sirens

In chapter 2 you learned that the anxious side screen gets your attention with a threat. Something you value in life feels like it is at risk—whether you're being perceived in a positive light, a loved one's safety, and so on. The *addictive* side screen, subject of this chapter, uses a different kind of hook. It gets your attention not with a threat but rather with an unhealthy temptation. You're hit with a craving for nicotine or a sugary treat. Driving home from work, your mind is bombarded with images of pouring the first drink. After putting the kids to bed, you go online and lose yourself for hours scrolling through and responding to social media posts.

When the addictive side screen lights up—especially when it shines brightly—you're in danger of being ensnared. If you're not alert, careful, and thoughtful, in terms of how you relate to the destructive enticement, you'll experience a loss of control. There's a tipping point where the drive to escape or satiate the desire takes over. For a brief period, when the addictive side screen has captivated your attention, you will go on autopilot, and the consequences of your actions will be far from your mind. Only later will you look back and wonder why you ate the whole bag of chips or spent needless hours surfing the Internet.

Most of us must, to one degree or another, contend with an addictive side screen. We're visited by urges and drawn away by alluring images and ideas that can cause us to act in some unhealthy ways. These temptations coming from the addictive side screen are hard to resist because they offer a chance to escape the stresses of life and make ourselves feel good. Wired to maximize pleasure and minimize pain, we can easily fall into a destructive pattern of using food, alcohol, social media, and other activities as a way to cope and self-soothe. These escapist behaviors, which can range from bad habits to full-blown addictions, can become deeply ingrained in our life and hard to change.

In this chapter, we explore how the addictive side screen operates in your life—when it tends to show up, how it tempts you, and the process by which you're seduced, resulting in a loss of control. And, most important, you'll see how to respond to the addictive side screen in a new way that will help you break the bad habit and bring about the desired change in your life.

How Is the Addictive Side Screen Unique?

Similar to the anxious side screen, the addictive side screen—and the destructive pull it generates on your mind—loses its power when you accept the presence of the challenging thoughts and feelings, while being diligent not to invest or focus on the content being displayed. This is Accept & Redirect, the first step of TSM that you've been learning. This response works because it deprives the side screen—the potentially destructive thoughts and feelings—of needed energy. Without the benefit of your attention and reactivity (resistance to the challenging internal activity), the side screen dims and fades into the background.

That said, each side screen has its particular challenges. With the anxious side screen, you feel under threat—a sense of danger and uncertainty is in the air. Reflexively, you'll try to avoid or escape the perceived threat, as well as the aversive feelings that go with this threat experience. Often this natural threat strategy takes the form of avoidance behaviors, whereby you stay away from those things in life that cause you to worry or feel anxious. As you learned in chapter 2, however, avoidance only creates more problems. It impairs your freedom and flexibility of choice, and you unknowingly invite more anxiety into your life, by confirming to the threat center of the brain that the avoided activity is indeed a genuine danger to you. Whenever you contemplate the given activity or get close to the avoided experience, your brain will sound the alarm with anxious thoughts and feelings. For this reason, successfully de-energizing the anxious side screen requires that you address the avoidance pattern. To help you accomplish this, you were introduced to the Freedom Ladder, a structured and systematic way of correcting avoidance behaviors.

In contrast, with the addictive side screen we're not concerned about avoidance behaviors or sending false, reinforcing messages to the threat center of the brain. In fact, the threat center of the brain isn't involved. The addictive side screen taps into the pleasure centers of the brain—the desire to feel good and keep feeling good—so it's often wise to take steps to avoid activating it in the first place. Unlike the anxious side screen, where the primary mission is learning how to move forward with your life while feeling under threat, the top priority with the addictive side screen is to protect your mind from being seduced— consumed and preoccupied with fulfilling the desire. There are specific strategies you can implement, both in advance and in the presence of tempting thoughts and feelings, that will help you successfully apply the principle of Accept & Redirect, allowing you to minimize the influence of the addictive side screen—and gain the freedom you seek.

Homer's Island of the Sirens

To guide you through the change process and show you how to apply TSM to break bad habits, we'll use an ancient Greek story as both a source of wisdom and an organizing structure for this chapter. This story effectively captures the destructive power of the addictive side screen, as well as the steps you can take to protect yourself. I'm referring to Homer's classic *The Odyssey*; in particular, his account of the Island of the Sirens.

The hero Odysseus and his men are on their homeward journey back to Ithaca. Off in the distance Odysseus spots the Island of the Sirens and recalls the warning he received from the Greek goddess Circe. The Sirens are beautiful sea creatures who lure men to their shores with bewitching music. When passing sailors hear the music, they're entranced. They impulsively jump off the ship and swim over to the rocky shores. Driven by intense desire, they are oblivious to the fact that the Sirens are man-eaters. Once the sailors reach the shores, they'll be torn up and devoured. Odysseus springs into action. He first instructs the crew to plug their ears with beeswax. Then he commands his men to tie him to the mast. As the knots are being tightened, he gives them a direct order: under no circumstances, no matter how much he begs, are they to untie the ropes.

Then it happens. Bound to the mast, Odysseus begins to hear the most enchanting music—the addictive side screen lights up. The pull is irresistible. Every fiber of his being wants to follow the seductive music to its source. He is taken over. Possessed by desire, Odysseus struggles against the ropes and demands to be released. But the crew remains faithful and only tightens the ropes. Soon the Island of the Sirens fades into the background and Odysseus returns to his senses. He raises an eyebrow, and his men run over to free their leader from the ropes. Odysseus has survived an encounter with the Sirens.

The addictive side screen is akin to the Island of the Sirens. You'll be in your car, at your computer, or walking down the street, when the side screen lights up and you hear the Sirens' song. It comes in the form of an urge or an idea or an enticing image. You'll feel like smoking a cigarette or visiting a website you know you shouldn't. It's good at grabbing your attention because it beckons with the promise of experiencing pleasure and escaping the stress or tedium of life. And similar to the sailors passing by the Island of the Sirens, if you entertain the temptation and lock into the music—if you give your attention to the side screen—you'll be overpowered and act in some unhealthy ways.

This tale of the Sirens, aside from demonstrating the destructive power of the addictive side screen, also reveals the steps you can take to break free and protect yourself from the Sirens' call. Embedded in Homer's account are four key principles—steps that, when followed, release you from the side screen's influence, thereby freeing you from the behavior pattern you're trying to break:

- **Anticipate the challenge.** Know when your addictive side screen tends to get activated.

- **Don't lock into the sirens' song!** Catch yourself watching the side screen early on, and apply Accept & Redirect.

- **Have accountability.** Use trusted others as support in the change process.

- **Redirect your life energy.** Find a healthy sanctuary for your mind in the midst of temptation.

In the following pages, you'll become familiar with these four key principles and learn how to apply them using TSM, so you can make the desired change in your life.

How Serious Is My Habit, and What Do I Call It?

How do we classify and measure the addictive side screen's influence in our life? In other words, when we're caught in a pattern of investing in the content showing up on the side screen and act in some unhealthy ways, what do we call the behavior? Is it just a bad habit? Is it an addiction? Or does it fall somewhere in between? If so, what do we call those behaviors?

In my clinical practice, I'm frequently asked to label a problem behavior. People want to gauge the seriousness of the behavior and know how concerned they should be. The spouse of a client will ask, "Does he have an addiction?" Or in session, a client will say, "I drink too much, but I don't think I'm an alcoholic... Do you think I'm an alcoholic?" Maybe you have similar questions. You know you engage in some unhealthy behaviors, but you're not sure what to call them—or how alarmed you should be.

This confusion is understandable because when it comes to conceptualizing and discussing destructive patterns of behavior, our vocabulary is limited. We use terms that are undefined and/or don't describe the complexities of our experience. We may have a general sense of what the everyday bad habit looks like and be able to spot an extreme addiction. But outside these clear-cut cases, it can be challenging to understand and classify the unhealthy patterns of behavior taking place in our own life.

To address this challenge, I find it helpful to think of *problem behaviors*, which is the general term I use to refer to all unhealthy behaviors, residing on a continuum, which is illustrated in figure 5.1. This scale offers a simple way of describing and measuring the severity of problem behaviors, which are divided into three categories: Bad Habits, Destructive Behaviors, and Addictive Behaviors.

1	2	3	4	5	6	7	8	9	10
BAD HABITS				DESTRUCTIVE BEHAVIORS				ADDICTIVE BEHAVIORS	

Figure 5.1: The Continuum of Unhealthy Behaviors

As you can see, the categories lie on a continuum scaled from 1 to 10, with 1 being the least severe and 10 being the most.

Severity here is measured in terms of the intensity of your cravings (how frequent and overwhelming is the urge?), compulsivity (how much control do you have over the behavior?), negative consequences (to what degree is the behavior negatively impacting your life, in terms of health, relationships, work, and so on?), and withdrawal symptoms (do you experience negative mental or physical symptoms when you abstain from the behavior?). On the lower end of the scale, these problems—cravings, compulsivity, and so on—are either not present or mild. In contrast, when your problem behavior falls farther to the right on the scale—moving closer to 10—these problems are pervasive, persistent, and severe. Let's take a closer look.

Beginning on the left side of the continuum, in the 0 to 3 range, you are in the realm of *bad habits*. A bad habit might be spending too much time on Facebook when really you should be either working or spending more time with those who are physically present. With a bad habit like this one, you know the behavior is less than ideal and doesn't represent your best—what you want for your life. And while you acknowledge it's a repetitive pattern of behavior, you don't experience strong or persistent cravings for Facebook—it's more something you do by default when bored or needing to unplug. And the negative fallout from the habit isn't significant. Once in a while your spouse may get mildly irritated, or occasionally you end up procrastinating on a work project. But you do know with a high degree of confidence that if you made it a priority you could stop.

As you move across the continuum, the equation begins to change. You leave the domain of bad habits and enter *destructive behaviors*, which lie on the scale between 4 and 7. In this zone, the addictive side screen becomes more active and influential. You begin to experience urges or cravings. You may even have bouts of losing control over the drinking, eating, or whatever the behavior might be—and usually with consequences. Maybe you show up late to a meeting or call in sick because of a hangover. Or the late-night binge eating takes you one step closer to diabetes, something your physician has warned you about and is monitoring closely.

Once you pass 7 and enter the far-right side of the continuum, you're in the domain of addiction. At this point, "getting the fix" (engaging in the behavior) becomes a primary preoccupation and organizing principle of your life, negatively impacting multiple life domains. Often your entire schedule outside of work revolves around easy access to alcohol or your drug of choice, while close relationships and activities outside of drinking cease to be as important. Or despite being in debt and having financial responsibilities to your family, you borrow money so you can gamble at the local horse track or casino. Even though a part of you may think you can stop or control the behavior, history has shown otherwise, and you've repeatedly had the experience of losing control—doing the very thing you promised yourself or a loved one you wouldn't do. And even if you take the difficult and courageous step of trying to stop the behavior, the body and mind resist. Your efforts will often be greeted with physical side effects such as shaking and sleepless nights, and psychological ones such as intense waves of anxiety and mood swings. In some cases, such as with opioids and alcohol, the withdrawal symptoms can even be life threatening.

Let's take a look at the behaviors you might be dealing with. (You can download a worksheet of this exercise at http://www.newharbinger.com/42327.)

LABEL YOUR BEHAVIOR

Refer back to figure 5.1. As you look at the scale, bring a problem behavior to mind. Maybe it's one of the ways you cope with anxiety or try to relax at night. After identifying the negative behavior—the one you know you need to change—examine and rate it on the 0 to 10 scale, using the following four domains of severity:

Intensity of urges/cravings   _____

Compulsivity (lack of control)   _____

Negative consequences   _____

Withdrawal symptoms   _____

Once you've assigned a number to each domain, you can add them up and divide by four to arrive at an average rating. This number will give you a general idea of how severe your problem behavior is and how to classify it in terms of bad habits, destructive behaviors, and addictive behaviors.

How did your behaviors rank? The Two-Screen Method can help you regardless of where you land on the problem behavior scale; this is true even for addictive behaviors. But there's one important disclaimer. If your problem has reached the level of an addiction (around 7 or higher on the scale), you'll likely need resources beyond TSM to break free. Individuals struggling with a bad habit or even a destructive behavior into the 5 to 6 range can often change on their own. This is rarely the case with addictions. Breaking free of addictive behaviors often requires a support structure that offers accountability, personal therapy, and a close community dedicated to your sobriety. TSM can play an important role in the process of recovering from addiction-level behavior, but it should be embedded in this larger treatment structure.

Breaking the Destructive Pattern

When Homer wrote the passage about the Sirens, it's doubtful he had the goal of helping people overcome problem behaviors. Intentions aside, Odysseus's brush with the Sirens contains all the ingredients for breaking a destructive behavior cycle. The story encapsulates the four key principles that protect you from being taken over by the addictive side screen—the culprit behind bad habits and destructive behaviors. The first step is anticipating the Island of the Sirens—predicting when your side screen tends to light up.

First Principle: Anticipate the Challenge

One of the first steps in breaking free from a bad habit or destructive behavior is identifying when and where you're most vulnerable. This is what Odysseus did when he took to heart Circe's warning that those who heard the Sirens' music would be overcome and never again return to loved ones. Recognizing the danger, Odysseus anticipated the challenge and took steps to protect himself.

In the same way, you anticipate the challenge by identifying the spaces and circumstances where you're most tempted to indulge in the unhealthy behavior. In other words, you get to know your addictive side screen and when it tends to show up. Karen, for example, is in the process of kicking a nicotine habit. She has a pretty good idea of when the cravings will come. Her challenge starts in the morning, when she's enjoying a cup of coffee. The side screen is automatically triggered with this morning ritual. She feels the urge to smoke and is visited by images of taking the first drag on the cigarette. And throughout the day, especially after a meal or during times of elevated stress, she's typically hit with cravings. She has also noticed that certain locations tend to light up her addictive side screen, such as the courtyard of her office building (where she used to smoke) and the local gas station where she bought smokes.

Now it's your turn. Take a moment to reflect on the particular problem behavior you want to change. As you bring it to mind, think of the *external* triggers—the common circumstances that surround the behavior and the environmental factors that make you feel most tempted to engage in it: time of day, day of the week, location, social context, and so on. Also, think of *internal* triggers—thoughts, feelings, and physical sensations that lead to the behavior you're trying to change. What are some of the emotions, such as sadness, loneliness, restlessness, boredom, or anxiousness, that trigger your addictive side screen? Go through a process of mapping out the vulnerable points in your life, where you're likely to engage in the problem behavior. Then write down the identified triggers here (or on the worksheet version of this exercise available at http://www.newharbinger.com/42327):

GETTING TO KNOW MY TRIGGERS

External Triggers: _____

Internal Triggers: _____

Identifying the external and internal triggers that prime you to engage in the bad habit or destructive behavior will help you predict and stay a few steps ahead of the temptation. This makes the addictive side screen less powerful, as it loses the element of surprise. When it shows up, you won't be thrown off balance. You'll experience a greater sense of control and capacity to make a healthy choice—to implement the steps you learn in this chapter.

Second Principle: Don't Lock into the Sirens' Song!

Odysseus has been warned of a sobering reality. The Sirens' music has the power to take over your mind and person. Once you lock into their song, you will lose control and be carried off to a destructive end.

This is a good analogy for how destructive behaviors get expressed in our life, where we go from a healthy place (not tempted and in touch with our values) to—inexplicably—repeating the same negative behavior. How does this happen? The process starts with a kind of seduction. The addictive side screen lights up, and an enticing thought or image comes into awareness. This is the Sirens' call. If you hang out and invest in the temptations flashing on the side screen, the free will window begins to close. Desire takes over. Your mind enters a state of preoccupation in which it's hard to focus on anything else. A funnel is created that channels your attention and guides you toward fulfilling the desire.

One of the easiest ways to protect yourself from being seduced is avoiding the Island of the Sirens altogether—minimizing your exposure to the triggers you identified in the previous section. If you're trying to curb your drinking, for example, it makes sense to avoid—when you can—situations where alcohol is the focus. Similarly, if you have a pattern of late-night snacking, you can help yourself by not purchasing the sweet and salty foods that offer the temptation.

Of course, you can't always avoid temptation. Inevitably, the addictive side screen will light up. Without a moment's notice, you'll find yourself staring at the side screen, craving nicotine or seeing the image of an irresistible piece of chocolate cake. When you find yourself in this vulnerable space, the key is to catch yourself watching the side screen as soon as possible and apply the first step of TSM. You accept the presence of the distracting temptations, along with the feelings of not satisfying the desire, while decisively planting your attention on the front screen.

> Tom is in treatment for sexual compulsivity, an addiction that has almost cost him his marriage. Freedom—and one of his treatment goals—includes not investing in the lustful thoughts and images that come into his mind throughout the day. He uses the two-screen image to understand what is happening in his mind and how to respond to the sexual temptations in a way that breaks the historical pattern.
>
> As he drives by a massage parlor he used to frequent, his addictive side screen gets triggered. A sexual experience from the past pops into his mind. Tom realizes he's watching the addictive side screen and quickly redirects his attention to the

road ahead, while allowing the side screen to run its tape in his peripheral vision. He knows acceptance doesn't mean he wants the sexual images to be there. Quite the opposite. He wants to be free of this compulsive pattern that has brought so much shame and pain into his and his family's life. If he had his way, he would take a baseball bat to the side screen and chase the lustful thoughts and images out of his mind. But he knows that trying to push the side screen out of awareness, which is what he wants to do, is a form of reactivity. He's learned that it will only cause the lustful thoughts and sexual images to become stronger and more likely to return. If Tom is interested in defusing the sexual content showing up on the side screen, the key is not fighting its presence but letting it be there while he channels his focus and life energy to the front screen. He keeps his eyes on the road, while listening to his favorite podcast.

In addition to applying the first step of TSM (Accept & Redirect) in the face of temptation, the Mindfulness Skills anchor, which you read about in chapter 4, can also be a valuable ally during these times of side screen activation. This anchor offers ideas and specific strategies for tethering your mind to the present moment, where it will be safe from the Sirens' call. You can use this anchor to open up your scope of awareness and attend to the world around you in the moment of temptation. You can even do a grounding exercise if you repeatedly find yourself being pulled back into the side screen, using one or more of the five senses (taste, touch, smell, sound, and sight) to hyperfocus on the external environment. Even doing this for a couple of minutes will turn down the volume on the Sirens' call.

Third Principle: Have Accountability

The third principle in breaking free from a destructive behavior is accountability. Odysseus modeled this by using his crew as a layer of protection from the Sirens. When he was in a centered, value-minded space, he talked to his men about the upcoming temptation and how they could help him. He even warned them about how he might act when under the Sirens' spell and how they could respond to keep him safe.

Whenever you try to build a new behavior or break a bad one, it's helpful to involve other people. Talk to a trusted friend or family member about your goals. Adding this simple step greatly increases your chance of success. When you commit yourself to an action publicly, it makes it harder to go back on that commitment, because someone besides you is watching for you to make a change—maybe even expecting or depending on it. This provides a disincentive to giving in to the temptation and also bolsters your resolve to make the healthy choice, which will later be celebrated.

Twelve-step groups, such as Alcoholic Anonymous (AA), are a good example of how accountability can be used to support change. Part of the group culture and expectation is that you find a sponsor—a group member who walks with you through the change process. Typically, there are brief weekly check-ins by phone and contact during anticipated or unanticipated times of temptation. If your family is gone for the weekend—something that is anticipated—maybe your sponsor calls you for a brief check-in on Friday and Saturday night, times when you're most apt to drink. The sponsor is also there for the unexpected times of temptation. Let's say you're on your way home from work and have an intense urge to stop at the local liquor store. Here, in this critical space with the addictive side screen shining brightly, there is a mutual understanding and agreement that you reach out to the sponsor. You call or send a text letting your sponsor know the space you're in. The sponsor does everything possible to be available during these times to help you navigate the temptation and make a healthy choice.

You don't have to suffer from alcoholism or some other diagnosable addiction to benefit from this model of accountability. Nor do you need to join a 12-step group. Instead, you can adopt and apply these accountability principles to your particular situation. For example, Karen, who's trying to give up cigarettes, has teamed up with a girlfriend who is also trying to break a bad habit. They both have shared the historical pattern around the behavior they're trying to change, as well as those times and situations when they experience the greatest temptation. With this information, they agreed on a communication structure—how frequently they will check in with each other and the medium of communication during times of temptation (call, text, email, and so on). Each makes a commitment to be a primary encourager and source of accountability through the change process.

No matter what recurring behavior you want to change, try to involve a trusted other who can offer support and accountability. It will greatly increase your chances of success.

Fourth Principle: Redirect Life Energy

The final principle is redirecting your life energy in the presence of the temptation. Odysseus's crew was enveloped in the Sirens' music. The only safeguard between them and the Sirens was a little beeswax. Plugging their ears was an important form of protection, but they went one step further. When faced with the danger, they implemented an action plan. Instead of focusing on the side screen temptation—the Island of the Sirens off in the distance—they went to work. They tended to the ship and watched over Odysseus, ensuring their leader's safety.

The addictive side screen is compelling. Once you hear the Sirens' call, it's easy to forget what's most important. Passing sailors, in a state of preoccupation, would momentarily forget that they were headed home to see loved ones. Once they were mesmerized by the addictive side screen, everything they cared about in life was pushed to the recesses of their minds. In that moment, their singular focus and mission was gratifying their desire. While your addictive side screen may not be as powerful or compelling as Homer's Sirens, you still need to safeguard yourself from its

negative influence. When it gets triggered, it presents an enticement that is hard to turn down. It beckons you with the promise
of pleasure and a needed escape from the stresses and responsibilities of life. To consistently say no to this temptation and to
break the bad habit, you need to find an alternative focus—with
sticking power—for your attention and life energy.

Finding these types of activities is the subject of the next
chapter. You will identify specific healthy activities that you can
move toward when the side screen is vying for your attention,
including times of temptation and overwhelming urges. The
Healthy Distractions and Activities (HDA) anchor, when used
this way, serves both a protective role, by keeping your eyes off the
side screen, and a life-enhancing role, by giving you the opportunity to redirect the side screen energy into a healthy form of aliveness, pleasure, or self-soothing.

Conclusion

The addictive side screen is the home of unhealthy temptations.
You'll be hit with a craving or the pull to escape—the chance to
feel good or to get away from the challenges of life. When these
temptations come into awareness, you are in danger of being
overtaken by the addictive side screen and repeating the destructive habit you're trying to change—overeating, losing yourself in
the Internet for hours, drinking too much, and so on.

To change a problem behavior, it's important to understand
how the addictive side screen operates in your life and begin relating to it in a new way that removes its power. Drawing from
Odysseus's experience with the Sirens, we highlighted four principles that help you break a bad habit or destructive behavior.
First, you figure out when your addictive side screen tends to light
up—*anticipate the challenge*—and when it does, prepare yourself
for wise action. When the temptations come, you make the internal commitment to keep your attention and life energy on the

front screen, while allowing the side screen to run its tape of temptations in your peripheral vision; that is, you *don't lock into the sirens' song* and you *redirect life energy* away from the side screen. And whenever possible, you invite into your change process trusted others who offer encouragement and supportive accountability (*have accountability*).

CHAPTER 6

HEALTHY DISTRACTIONS AND ACTIVITIES ANCHOR Sanctuary for the Vulnerable Mind

With the Two-Screen Method, your relationship with the side screen is guided by the principle of Accept & Redirect. You first accept the presence of the anxious thoughts and feelings that show up on the side screen, without debating the worries or trying to escape the uncomfortable experience. You accept the nervous energy in your body, instead of fighting the feeling or focusing on it. This principle of acceptance is critical, because it's the opposite of reactivity—a primary energy source for anxious worries and destructive moods. By accepting the unwelcome thoughts and feelings on the side screen—the worries, the overwhelming feelings—you ultimately decrease their presence and power.

The second facet of your relationship with the side screen is redirecting attention to the front screen. Acceptance protects you from energizing the side screen through reactivity, but it doesn't address the second way that worries, anxiety, and other destructive feelings can be strengthened: through your attention. After you've accepted the presence of the hard thoughts and feelings, you need a home for your attention and life energy that isn't the side screen, so you can shift your focus off the side screen and deprive it of this second energy source.

If you've started applying TSM, you've probably noticed that redirecting attention away from the side screen can be challenging. Even when you make every effort to apply acceptance to a worrisome thought or painful feeling, your mind can still be drawn back to the side screen. Psychologically, emotionally, it will feel as if the side screen requires your attention—that you *must* monitor or resolve it. To override this reflexive response, you need an effective hook for your attention.

Recognizing this challenge, TSM offers three anchors designed to tether your attention to the front screen. The first one, Mindfulness Skills, was covered in chapter 4. As you read, one of the best and most effective steps you can take when feeling worried or emotionally overwhelmed is to bring your mind and person into awareness of the present moment, a primary goal of mindfulness. The Mindfulness Skills anchor helps you cultivate this ability. As we discussed, you can't be in the present moment and focused on the side screen at the same time. These two mental activities are neurologically incompatible. Therefore, the more capacity you develop in bringing awareness into the present moment, the less powerful and influential the side screen becomes.

In this chapter, we'll look at the Healthy Distractions and Activities (HDA) anchor. You'll be taken through a process of identifying healthy, life-giving activities you can invest in when your mind is drawn to the side screen. While the primary goal of the HDA anchor is to protect you from energizing the side screen with your attention, it can also be used to improve your quality of life. You can choose activities that do more than distract you from the side screen. In this chapter, you'll identify *physical activities*, *pleasurable activities*, and *enlivening activities* that can be used for this front screen anchor. These type of activities, as you will discover, can meet important needs in your life that are currently unmet, such as the need for positive self-soothing and excitement, and introduce more vitality into your daily life. In short, with the HDA anchor you can use the presence of challenging thoughts and feelings—showing up on the side screen—as a reminder and opportunity to positively move your life forward.

Isn't Distraction a Form of Avoidance?

Before we begin, let's take a moment to clarify the function of the HDA anchor and how you'll apply it.

In articles or other books on mindfulness, it's doubtful you will encounter distraction as a recommended strategy. Traditionally, from a mindfulness perspective, the idea of distracting yourself could be viewed as a form of avoidance—an attempt to escape painful thoughts and feelings. Mindfulness is about creating space for, and not fighting or running from, challenging internal experiences. It's about letting go of mastery and control—whereby you try to dictate and shape life's experiences to your comfort level—and shifting into a disposition of openness and acceptance of what is happening in the present moment, including uncomfortable or even painful experiences. On the surface, then, this idea of using the HDA anchor to distract yourself from anxious thoughts and feelings seems incongruent with the standard mindfulness approach.

This would be true if you were encouraged to distract yourself without *also* applying mindful acceptance. But you're not being encouraged to push the side screen—the worry, the anxious feeling—out of awareness or to escape it through the use of a distraction. In TSM, distraction—as applied with the HDA anchor—is always used in conjunction with acceptance. If you begin worrying unnecessarily about a loved one's safety, for example, you first employ the principle of acceptance. As difficult as it is, you don't fight or run from the troubling thoughts that something bad could happen to your friend or family member. You make space for the feeling of uncertainty and vulnerability. You do your best to let go internally, allowing the side screen to freely run its tape.

Once you've applied acceptance, you need to shift gears and move on with your life. There's nothing more to understand or resolve on the side screen. The challenging thoughts and feelings are there, actively displayed on the side screen, and now the task is to find a safe home for your mental attention. If you don't, you'll be drawn back into the same recycled worries from which you're seeking freedom. Once you have applied acceptance, a healthy distraction can be helpful, not as a form of avoidance, but as a strategy to protect you from getting entangled in thoughts and feelings that add no value to your life—the side screen activity that interferes with enjoying your life—and to find some internal peace.

Let's take it one step further. The HDA anchor can actually stretch or increase your capacity for mindful acceptance by giving you a structured way to practice one of the most unnatural and challenging psychological tasks: moving forward with your life and attention while feeling under threat. If you're worried that some negative event could befall a loved one, whatever the fear might be, you'll be reluctant to redirect your attention away from that concern on the side screen. If you run into a friend at the supermarket, your attention will be divided. Even when you know it's an irrational fear, you'll be drawn to attend to the worries scrolling across the side screen. It will feel unwise—maybe irresponsible—to be fully present with your friend and leave the potential threat on the side screen unattended and unresolved. It would feel like the equivalent of reading a magazine on your couch while the house is on fire. You want to put out those flames!

With anxiety, however, it only *feels* like the house is on fire—there is no genuine threat, only the feeling. What you need to do is move forward with your life as if there were no threat, even though that's exactly how you feel—under threat! This is a challenging psychological experience to take on and accept. The HDA anchor can help you accomplish this task.

Four Types of Healthy Distractions and Activities

Let's get into the specifics of the HDA anchor and how to apply it. To make full use of this anchor, you'll want to generate a diverse list of healthy distractions you can use for a variety of situations and needs. And to help you develop such a list, you'll be introduced to four main types of healthy distraction activities: *physical, pleasurable, enlivening,* and *general.* As you read through each type, you'll be encouraged to generate some possible activities that would be useful in that category. Write down potential activities for each of the four types—either on a separate piece of paper, or using the worksheet available at http://www.newharbinger.com/42327—and you'll have a rich list of activities to choose from when you need to apply the HDA anchor. The goal, by the chapter's end, is for you to have a useful list of activities that can help you navigate anxious and other challenging spaces, while—at least at times—fulfilling an important need, such as feeling more alive or joyful or increasing your ability to de-stress.

Physical Activities

When the side screen is vying for your attention, one of the most effective distractions is physical exercise. You go for a run or a swim or take a vigorous walk that takes your mind off the side screen. One benefit of this HDA, beyond the obvious health benefits, is the natural way it redirects your life energy. When you're investing in anxious thoughts on the side screen, your attention and life energy are turned inward. To break free of the worries, and to avoid getting stuck in a destructive feeling, you need to shift this inward focus. Physical activities naturally rotate your attention and life energy outward, moving awareness away from the side screen.

Exercise also has significant mood benefits. Part of this comes from the chemicals released in the body during and after physical activity. After a good workout, hormones and neurochemicals, such as endorphins and dopamine, generate relaxation, pleasure, and a sense of well-being. And a secondary source of well-being is the personal satisfaction of doing something healthy. After the hike, run, or spin class, you feel a sense of accomplishment. This creates a positive feedback loop: you feel better about yourself, which makes you more likely to engage in the activity associated with the positive feeling, generating an ever-increasing sense of well-being.

Exercise is also good for breaking down and metabolizing nervous energy and other restless internal states. At times you need to discharge pent-up energy. Maybe you've had a stressful day at work and your mind is already racing about the pressures of tomorrow. Or maybe you're feeling consumed by an unhealthy urge, finding it hard to focus on anything but the website you want to visit or the dessert you want to consume. You can get substantial relief through exercise. It will help you work through and release the pent-up energy of these charged internal states—the stress, the anxious feeling, the craving. And the soothing sensation that often follows exercise gives you further physical and emotional relief.

Take a moment to reflect on possible physical activities that could serve as a healthy distraction in your life. These could be swimming; running; stretching; dancing to your favorite music; going for a walk, hike, or bike ride; gardening; or yoga—anything that gets your body moving and blood pumping. Try to identify at least four physical activities and write them down.

Pleasurable Activities

On your list of potential HDAs, it's good to include some activities that contain a degree of pleasure. This is especially true if lack of pleasure—having regular experiences of feeling good—is part of your struggle. Depressed moods, for example, interfere with the experience of pleasure. In the extreme, as with clinical depression, a person can experience something called *anhedonia*—a complete inability to feel pleasure. Nothing in life feels good, not even those activities that used to be pleasurable. Understandably, a life void of pleasure has natural implications. You stop looking forward to things. You lose motivation to stay active—to go out with friends, work out, stay on top of your responsibilities, and so on. Your life turns from color to black-and-white.

Wherever you fall on the mood scale, if you run low in the pleasure department, the HDA anchor can help. The same activity you select as a healthy distraction from the side screen can also tap into the pleasure centers of the brain, giving you a much-needed boost. Clinicians sometimes refer to these activities as dopamine spikes. Dopamine is one of the neurochemicals in the brain associated with pleasure. When you engage in certain kinds of activities—such as taking a walk around the city, meeting a close friend for lunch, or dancing to your favorite music—the brain releases dopamine and other mood-enhancing neurotransmitters, and both your mood and your outlook on life brighten.

HDAs that offer pleasure are also important when trying to change a bad habit or destructive behavior (the addictive side screen). Tom, in chapter 5, suffered from sexual compulsivity, and one of his treatment goals was abstaining from internet pornography, an unhealthy preoccupation that threatened his marriage. Incorporating healthy pleasurable activities into his life played an important role in breaking the destructive pattern. In conjunction with physical activities (reviewed in the preceding section), Tom found ways to experience pleasure and fulfill important needs that didn't put a strain on his marriage or compromise his values. Let's take a look at how he employed the HDA anchor.

Tom recognized that he was most vulnerable to watching internet porn after 9:00 p.m., a time when the rest of the family was in bed and he was in a depleted state after a long day of work and family responsibilities. To make a change and disrupt the old pattern, he needed an alternative home for his attention and life energy in the evening. Telling himself *Don't look at porn!* wasn't enough—he had already tried this approach many times. Instead, he needed a new set of activities that not only captured his attention but also met some of the needs fulfilled by the destructive behavior. Tom's use of porn came at a cost—to his marriage, to how he felt as a person following the activity—but it did meet some short-term needs. In the moment, when Tom was engaged in the behavior, he experienced pleasure, soothing, stimulation, and a break from the stresses of life. These underlying need states and his desire to fulfill them were not necessarily unhealthy. The problem was the way Tom went about fulfilling them. He needed to find other methods—healthy substitutes—for feeling good and getting a much-needed break from life stressors.

With this goal in mind, Tom reviewed his HDA list and selected *swimming, listening to music,* and *working on a jigsaw puzzle* for his HDA anchor. At 9:00 p.m., Tom pulled on his swim trunks and went to the community pool for a swim. This physical activity allowed him to de-stress and experience some healthy self-soothing. After returning from the pool, he had roughly one hour before he was ready for bed. He spent the remaining hour in the dining room, surrounded by family pictures and colorful artwork. There he listened to his favorite tunes—a significant source of pleasure—and worked on the thousand-piece family jigsaw puzzle (another source of positive pleasure and stimulation) until it was time for bed.

With this new evening ritual, the old space that used to be filled with internet porn was now occupied with healthy activities that boosted his mood, stimulated his mind, and kept his attention off the side screen. As Tom applied the HDA anchor, he still had to deal with sexual urges, as well as tempting thoughts and images popping into his mind. This was especially true in the first month. But instead of allowing his mind to drift with the sexual content, he practiced redirecting his attention back to the music, back to the puzzle. He also found it helpful to switch up and experiment with other new healthy distractions, such as curling up with a good book or practicing different mindfulness meditations, which were equally effective in holding his attention. He also worked on redirecting his sexual energy into healthy physical intimacy with his wife. Consequently, his wife felt more desired in the relationship—a previously unmet need—and Tom discovered a new level of intimacy and pleasure with his wife of twenty years.

All the while, as the weeks and months passed, his compulsive desire to view porn steadily decreased, as did his need for a regimented schedule each evening.

Regardless of the particular struggle you're trying to address, you will likely benefit from adding some pleasurable activities to your personal HDA list. You want your list to be well rounded, containing a range of healthy distractions and activities you can use for a variety of needs and purposes. Similar to what you did for physical activities, try to identify some pleasurable activities. What healthy activities do you take pleasure in? It could be watching your favorite comedy and getting a good laugh, or playing a board game with friends. Maybe it's picking up your guitar and strumming a few chords, or singing in the shower. Take a moment and think about those times—those activities—that have generated positive or soothing feelings. Try to write down at least four possibilities.

Enlivening Activities

Now we turn to a third type, *enlivening activities*. As the name suggests, this type of HDA goes well beyond providing safe harbor from the side screen. Enlivening activities inject aliveness into your bloodstream, generating excitement or joy or a more vibrant connection with life. This can be a powerful way to use the HDA anchor, where the anxious feeling or unhealthy urge—the challenging side screen activity—leads you to an activity that helps you feel more alive. While the experience of aliveness can't be reduced to a simple formula, there are ways to cultivate it and set the stage for its arrival. People often experience aliveness when they appropriately *challenge* themselves, experience a sense of *adventure*, or tap into their *creativity*. In this next section, beginning with the theme of challenge, we'll explore the reliable sources of positive stimulation and aliveness that make up the enlivening distraction type.

CHALLENGE

For starters, challenging yourself is a highly effective way of diverting your attention away from the side screen. When you face a healthy challenge, whether it be taking that intimidating workout class or trying to do a minor household repair, you can't afford to go away in your mind and hang out with the worries or unsettling feelings showing up on the side screen. The current challenge naturally demands your complete focus. Your brain, aware of this requirement, comes to your aid by unleashing greater attentional powers, so your mind is unusually focused on fixing the household appliance or following the instructor's movements in that newly offered aerobics class. Whatever the challenge, you will notice an increased capacity to stay focused on what you're doing in that moment, which means you're not watching the side screen.

And, in keeping with this category, a challenging activity can bring more aliveness into your life. It's an antidote to the stale, predictable life pattern that many of us fall into. Try to find ways to stretch yourself in small ways each week. Maybe you learn a new chord on the piano or research an important public policy issue that has left you confused. Then once a month or quarter, take a stab at a bigger challenge. Go for the more challenging bike ride or hike. Download a foreign language app or sign up for Toastmasters. As you're generating ideas for the enlivening category, try to include some activities that tap into this challenge theme.

ADVENTURE

The opposite of the daily grind is adventure, another common channel for aliveness. Similar to a challenge, an adventurous activity breaks up the monotony and expands your life sphere. It stimulates your senses with something new and exciting. Your brain, which loves to process new stimuli, will naturally be more present-moment-focused as it soaks in the novel sights, sounds, and sensations. This automatic response to adventure is one reason why some people are surprised by a decrease in worry and anxiety when visiting a new area or country. It would be easy to expect the opposite—that leaving the familiar and venturing into the unknown would make people more anxious. But usually it's not the case, because the mind is so busy and distracted by taking in the new experience that there is little time for or interest in watching the side screen. The side screen can't compete with the new landscape, the fresh faces, the historical sites, and the unfamiliar cuisine.

Think of a couple of activities that would fall in the adventure category—something that breaks the routine and gives you a chance to explore. Keep in mind, an adventurous activity doesn't have to be backpacking in the Himalayas. It could be preparing or trying a new cuisine or volunteering at the local homeless shelter. The key is exploring new experiences that tap into your sense of adventure.

CREATIVITY

The other theme to keep in mind for *enlivening activities* is creativity. This part of self, the creative side, is often neglected in adulthood. As the responsibilities mount and our lives become more complex, it's easy to fall into a pattern of efficiency and productivity. There is always something to do—at work, with the kids, around the house. When a free space does open up, your first impulse may be to collapse on the nearest couch to catch your breath. While there may be many fixed aspects to your daily and weekly routine—things you can't change—it's still advisable, and probably doable, to find small ways to express your creative side. It will feed a part of you that normal life activities can't— and give you the needed energy to keep up with a busy life.

As you read this, you may wonder whether you're a creative person. If this question is running through your mind, you may need to expand your definition of creativity. Creativity isn't just for the painters and poets. There are many ways to express creativity. Cooking can be a creative endeavor; so can planning a trip or arranging flowers or blogging. But don't be intimidated by the traditional forms of creativity either. It could be fun to experiment with sketching or painting or writing a poem. You don't necessarily have to be "good" at the particular activity as long as it's enjoyable and provides enough stimulation to hold your attention. Explore and work on expressing this part of yourself by trying different creative tasks.

Now it's time for you to generate some ideas for this enlivening category. Holding in mind the themes of challenge, adventure, and creativity, list some possibilities you could imagine trying out or incorporating into your life. Keep in mind you can always add to or modify your list later. Right now you're looking for a few activities to get you started.

General Activities

This final category is for those activities that are good at holding your attention but don't fit neatly into one of the preceding categories. Some people, for example, will stay focused and engaged when planning a trip but the experience doesn't rise to the level of pleasure or creativity. The activity is mildly enjoyable, or emotionally neutral, yet holds your attention. You may find that cleaning or organizing or helping out the kids with homework falls into this category. For whatever reason, the given activity—maybe because it's important to you—naturally and easily holds your attention. Take a moment to add some healthy distractions that fall into this more general category; aim for at least four.

The bottom line is this: any activity, providing it's not harmful, that is an effective tether for your mind is a potential candidate for your HDA list.

Activating the HDA Anchor

So far in this chapter, we've been discussing four types of activities that can be used in your application of the HDA front screen anchor. I hope that at this point you have a working draft of at least sixteen activities, drawing from each distraction type. You now have a rich pool of healthy distractions from which to draw, depending on the situation and the kind of help you need.

Sometimes your use of this anchor will be fairly straightforward. In response to worries or an overwhelming feeling, you engage in a healthy distraction. Let's say it's Sunday afternoon and you start worrying about an interview you have the following day. *What if I don't know how to answer one of the questions? What if I stumble over my words or they see how nervous I am?* Instead of investing in the worrisome thoughts, you apply Accept & Redirect. You accept the nervous feeling, as well as the presence of the unwelcome thoughts, while reminding yourself to stay on the front screen. To help you employ the second step of TSM, staying tethered to the front screen, you engage in a healthy distraction from your list. You decide to do some gardening (*pleasurable activity*) in the backyard. In this scenario, gardening for an hour or so may be all that you need to manage the anxiety in a healthy way.

Alternatively, you can plan in advance to use the HDA anchor at times when you know you'll be vulnerable to an unhealthy temptation or anxious trigger. This is how Tom used the HDA anchor. He anticipated the challenge in advance and systematically implemented activities from his HDA list when entering the vulnerable time, which was around 9:00 p.m.

On other occasions, the HDA anchor can function more as a self-care plan to protect your mood or introduce more aliveness into your life. An executive I worked with suffered from chronic stress, bouts of mild depression and anxiety, and a general lack of passion and life purpose. One way he addressed this problem was with the HDA anchor. He scheduled a variety of activities— actually put them on his Google calendar—that he followed religiously for two months. Each week he took a guitar lesson, went for several jogs, learned one new thing daily (vocabulary word, historical fact, someone's name, and so on), spent time in the hot tub, and went on a Friday date night with his wife. Each week, in combination with the other TSM front screen anchors (Mindfulness Skills and Loving Action—more on that in chapter 8), his stress got lower, his mood improved, and he was less susceptible to dips into depression.

At times you'll need the HDA anchor to help you in all three areas where it's helpful—when you face a challenge that requires you to respond to unexpected side screen activation and to address known times of vulnerability, and when you need a general self-care plan. To illustrate, let's examine how you might use the HDA anchor in this more comprehensive way to address a fear of flying.

Applying the HDA Anchor to an Anxious Experience

Let's say you recently had one of the worst—most terrifying—flights of your life. The turbulence was so bad that overhead bins were popping open and many passengers used the airsick bags. Following this experience, your historic discomfort with flying became a full-blown fear. You'd be happy if you never set foot on an aircraft again—and secretly hope this will be the case.

After months of doing everything in your power to stay off planes, a critical work meeting or an important family celebration on the other coast forces you to fly.

The first issue to be addressed is anticipatory anxiety—the worry and anxiety you experience leading up to the trip. Aware that the flight is coming, your mind will want to brood over the feared event in advance. You might imagine being trapped on the plane in the midst of a panic attack. You may wonder how torturous the anxiety will be and whether or not you can handle it. You may worry about making a scene or losing your mind, as images of running up and down the aisle, screaming, flash through your mind.

This anticipatory anxiety tends to build as you get closer to the actual day of travel, showing up in the evenings or other times during the day when there are fewer distractions. One very helpful step you can take is increasing your physical exercise. In addition to being a healthy distraction, exercise helps break down and metabolize the nervous energy that accompanies anticipatory anxiety. When an anxiety-producing event is on the horizon, whether it's flying or public speaking or going on a date, it's a good idea to review your list of physical activities and make a plan. Identify what the physical exercise will be and when it will happen. It's important to put these HDAs on your schedule and treat them as appointments.

In addition to regular exercise, you'll want to identify some healthy distractions—most likely for the evening—that naturally hold your attention and, if at all possible, are soothing. Maybe it's taking a hot bath or watching your favorite comedy. Maybe there's an art project or creative task you'd like to work on that would protect your mind from drifting over to the side screen and worrying. Along those lines, one possible application of the HDA anchor for anticipatory anxiety could be: 6:00 p.m., jogging or yoga class; 8:00 to 9:00 p.m., favorite sitcom; 9:00 p.m., hot bath before bed.

The anticipatory anxiety will also be present driving to the airport, checking in, going through security, and waiting to board. In these situations, you may not be able to use many of your healthy distractions. No jogging or hot baths can happen between your leaving your home and boarding the aircraft. Yet you still need to protect your mind from investing in the side screen worries. If you don't have access to helpful HDAs in the moment, your best strategy is to hyperfocus on the external world—a technique covered in chapter 4. As you walk through the airport, you intensely focus on what is happening around you. Notice what people are wearing; study the color and patterns of the clothing. Take note of the sounds and scents as you pass by the shops and restaurants. Notice how your feet feel as they make contact with the ground or how the carryon strap feels on your shoulder.

Once you're on the plane, it's time to implement your well-thought-out distraction plan. In advance of the flight, you identify specific activities that have the best chance of holding your attention in the midst of the anxious experience. In the absence of a healthy distraction, you'll be prone to anxious hypervigilance. Similar to an alarmed cat with its back arched, you will feel impelled to stand guard and monitor everything that is happening—the movement and sounds of the aircraft, the flight attendants' facial expressions, the out-of-control feeling in your body. Instead of going down this path, which will keep you suspended in an anxious state, you implement the HDA anchor. You make a concerted and repeated effort to keep your internal eyes on the front screen by engaging in a healthy distraction. You take some deep breaths and start reading the novel or interesting magazine you brought. You get out the Sudoku or crossword puzzle. And throughout the flight (or whatever the anxious activity happens to be) you rely on the hyperfocus technique as needed. If the anxiety reaches a point where you can't focus on the healthy distraction, take a couple of minutes and listen intently to the sounds in the environment or study something visually. After hyperfocusing for a few minutes, remind yourself to accept the anxious experience and return to the HDA.

Conclusion

In this chapter, you were introduced to the second front screen anchor, Healthy Distractions and Activities (HDA). We reviewed four main types of healthy distraction activities you can use in response to challenging thoughts and feelings: physical, pleasurable, enlivening, and general. Along the way, you were encouraged to work on your own personalized list of healthy distractions that will be helpful for your particular needs and issues of concern.

Finally, we looked at applying them in some real-life situations. You observed the different ways you could employ the HDA anchor to handle anxiety-inducing situations from the fairly simple and straightforward to more complex ones.

Having your HDA anchor up and running will be a valuable and needed resource if you're challenged by the side screen we'll cover in the next chapter: the depressive side screen. Let's take a look.

CHAPTER 7

THE DEPRESSIVE
SIDE SCREEN
The Dark Seducer

Imagine walking into a movie theater and finding the best seat in the house. The lights dim, you slip on your 3D glasses, and the movie begins. The film is about your life. The screen is filled with familiar images and experiences. You see scenes from your childhood and adult life. You see in vivid color those important events that have shaped you as a person through the years. The movie you're watching even runs beyond the present to give you a glimpse into the future.

So far this may not sound too bad, but I've withheld an important detail. The film you're watching is an extremely negative take on your life. It's a dark drama. You see all the mistakes. All the times you failed as a person. The images on the screen fill you with guilt and regret. It's painful to watch. You see the times you were rejected and felt unloved. And as if this were not punishment enough, the movie director is known for juxtaposing the life of the main character—you—with the lives of others. The film periodically cuts from your depressing, unfulfilled life to other characters' full, happy lives.

How do you think you would feel after watching this movie for six hours? Twelve hours? What state would you be in after sitting there for two weeks, watching a depressing storyline about your life hour after hour, day after day? One word immediately comes to mind: *depressed!* In fact, I doubt you'd need days or even hours in this theater for your mood to darken. It would happen quickly. It might take only a few minutes of starring at the big screen before you started to feel the effects. The images parading across the screen would rapidly change your mood. Any good feelings and positive aspects of your life would vanish from your awareness, leaving you with a depressed feeling and dark outlook on life.

While this movie theater experience may seem a little far-fetched, it's actually a good description of what can happen in your internal world. Without realizing it, you can go away in your mind and spend hours entertaining negative thoughts about yourself, remembering past hurts, and imagining a gloomy future—all of which have natural consequences for your mood and overall sense of well-being.

Unique Features of the Depressive Side Screen

Each type of side screen we've looked at has its unique features and challenges. To break free of the *anxious side screen,* for example, you need to override your protective instincts—the impulse to either avoid or become preoccupied with the anxious worries coming into awareness. Instead of trying to resolve the threats—the anxious feeling, the alarming thoughts—announcing themselves on the side screen, the path to freedom entails placing your attention on the front screen, while accepting the presence of these anxious worries (psychological threats) in your peripheral vision (side screen). Stated more broadly, your challenge, if you want to make the anxious side screen less powerful in your life, is learning how to move forward with your life, even while feeling under threat on an emotional and psychological level.

The *addictive side screen,* in contrast, isn't about feeling threatened or feeling that something of value is at risk. Instead, you're presented with a destructive enticement, an unhealthy urge. Here the challenge is passing up on the opportunity to feel pleasure or escape pain. As we discussed in chapter 5, it's critical, once the addictive side screen has been activated, to redirect your attention as soon as possible. Taking quick action will safeguard your mind from entering a state of preoccupation. More so than with the other side screens, the free will window, in which you have the freedom to make a healthy choice, closes rapidly. Once you lock into the Sirens' music—mentally invest in the tempting thoughts and feelings—you'll find it difficult, if not impossible, to resist the powerful current carrying you toward the destructive behavior.

The *depressive side screen*, the focus of this chapter, also has its unique features and challenges. One major difference is its subtle nature and how it can be up and running without your even realizing it. This is different from the anxious and addictive side screens, which often announce themselves with great fanfare. You know when you're anxious or can't let go of a worry; the same is true for a craving or destructive urge showing up on the addictive side screen. There may be a progression, where the anxious feeling or cravings are more subtle at first, but, for the most part, these side screens make themselves known—which also allows you to intervene early on in the process, right after the anxious or addictive side screen is activated.

In contrast, the depressive side screen can be hard to detect. You can be investing in side screen thoughts without knowing it. And by the time the depressed mood arrives, it's often too late. The way you feel and see the world has changed. You lose the motivation to take healthy action.

How the Depressive Side Screen Shows Up

The depressive side screen is easy to overlook because of its subtle, incremental nature. It doesn't blare messages from a loudspeaker so its presence—and the depressive content it generates—is easily detected. Instead, the depressive side screen, especially in the early stages, lurks in the recesses of your mind. Hidden from view, it starts whispering dark thoughts into awareness:

| You're a loser. Nobody likes you. |
| You'll always be alone. You don't deserve [whatever the good thing is]. |
| Your life will always be bad. You've always been missing something. |

These negative thoughts coming into awareness may not have much impact at first. But if you invest in them mentally—if you listen to and internalize these thoughts as objective reality and immerse yourself in memories and ideas that support these negative beliefs—your mood will shift. Your view of self and the life you're living will change. Without even knowing when or how it happened, you find yourself stuck and weighed down by a depressed mood. You may still be able to function—go to work, take care of the kids, and so on—but without contentment or positive feelings. The activities of daily life register as a chore, requiring energy that's hard to muster. Once you enter this emotional space, you can't even pretend to cheer yourself up or put a positive spin on life; the negative feeling is too strong, too convincing. And when you have unknowingly been investing in the depressive side screen, you may not be able to see or locate the front screen. The only screen in view is the depressive side screen. All you can see is the depressing movie about your life.

Striking a New Relationship with the Depressive Side Screen

In this chapter, you'll learn how to detect the presence of the depressive side screen and respond to it in a way that will protect your mood and cultivate a sense of well-being. To accomplish this, you'll first become familiar with the type of ideas and thoughts the depressive side screen tends to generate. As you'll see, identifying these unhealthy thought patterns common to the side screen provides you with an early warning system. It enables you to see when the depressive side screen shows up, even at lower levels of activation, so you don't invest in the thoughts that give it energy and deflate your mood. Then, after equipping you with this early detection system, the chapter will focus on two other critical tasks in managing your moods and feeling good: staying active despite what you're feeling, and tethering your mind to the external world and present moment.

The Connection Between Thoughts and Mood

For centuries, scholars, philosophers, and practitioners of various kinds have been interested in understanding and treating negative mood states. However, the real breakthrough didn't occur until the cognitive revolution of the 1950s and 1960s. This was a movement in academic and scientific psychology that explored how thinking styles and thought patterns contributed to people's mental and emotional well-being. A primary focus of this research was depression. Pioneers in the field, such as Aaron Beck and David Burns, discovered a strong link between depressed moods and thinking styles. People suffering from depressive symptoms tend to commit a predictable set of thinking errors or cognitive distortions that give rise to or perpetuate negative mood states. Further, and most importantly, researchers found that mood problems can be changed—alleviated—by altering these unhealthy ways of thinking. Thus cognitive therapy was born.

In his book *Feeling Good* (1980), Burns outlines ten cognitive distortions—ways of thinking—that support a depressed mood. He then guides the reader through the process of monitoring and recording thought patterns over several weeks, so you can see when you're engaging in one of these cognitive distortions. The idea is to raise awareness of when you're committing a cognitive distortion so you can replace it with a healthier, more accurate thought that protects the mood. This approach to problematic moods folds naturally into TSM and its emphasis on de-energizing destructive thoughts and feelings through the removal of mental investment—that is, watching the side screen. Watching for the cognitive distortions contained in depressive thought patterns can protect you from investing in the depressive side screen and darkening your mood. If you become familiar with these cognitive distortions and how they tend to show up in your mind, you have a built-in warning system, alerting you to the depressive side screen's presence.

Recognizing Depressive Side Screen Content

In this section, you'll be introduced to the six most common cognitive distortions that can alert you to the side screen's presence. They encapsulate the majority of cognitive beliefs and unhealthy thinking patterns that feed negative moods. These six, however, are not intended to be a comprehensive list of cognitive distortions. Other cognitive-behavioral practitioners would likely outline more than six; Burns himself lists ten in his bestselling book previously mentioned. However, there's a lot of overlap among the various cognitive distortions, as the unhealthy thinking pattern involves multiple cognitive distortions and doesn't fall neatly into one category. The goal of this chapter is to equip you with the essentials, so you can see when the depressive side screen is activated. The six we're about to review accomplish this objective.

ALL-OR-NOTHING THINKING

With this cognitive error, the world and self are viewed as either *all good* or *all bad*. There is no gray. You are either a success or a total failure. Your life is either good and worth living or completely miserable and worthless, with nothing in between.

Interestingly enough, the people I know who tend to commit this thinking error, at least in the context of depression, rarely experience the *all good* side of the equation. Theoretically, at least in a fair universe, the *all good* and *all bad* would be portioned out equally. Some days you would feel like the best employee ever and other days you would feel like the worst. But rarely does it work that way. If the *all good* side of the pendulum is experienced, it is short lived. Most of the time the person is stuck in the *all bad* camp, which fuels a depressed mood.

Usually this all-or-nothing thinking gets expressed in the form of perfectionism. The person believes or feels that he has to be perfect. If he's perfect, then he gets to experience being all good. One minor slip-up, however, drops below the perfectionistic standard and is experienced as total and complete failure. Any instance when he's not perfect confronts him with a damaged self-concept—a deep feeling that he's less-than and worthless. The drive toward perfectionism is the person's attempt to cover up this wounded self and keep it at bay.

You can see how the drive toward perfectionism is problematic. You set yourself up for the experience of failure, which only confirms and reinforces your negative self view. You won't always get a perfect score in a performance review, or in your grades at school; it's impossible to live and perform absolutely perfectly. And there are many areas of life where measuring performance is highly subjective. How, for example, do you measure your performance as a spouse or a friend? In these domains, perfection is elusive and unattainable. Ultimately, you have to change the underlying assumptions that give birth to perfectionism and the all-or-nothing thinking style.

A graduate student I worked with was highly perfectionistic and regularly engaged in all-or-nothing thinking. In her mind, only a 95 percent or higher was acceptable. Anything less and she was overwhelmed with a sense of failure and panic. We used her goal-oriented personality to chip away at the perfectionism and prevent her from energizing the depressive side screen. We framed success as *striving to be average*. As a treatment intervention, she approached her courses with the goal of mediocrity. Her mission was to be the good-enough student. Each morning she uttered the humorous mantra, "Today I'm going to be the best mediocre student I can be." This approach introduced some levity and allowed her to defuse the perfectionistic (all-or-nothing) thinking. She also discovered that her feelings of failure were highly exaggerated and not a good measurement of her performance. There were times when she was convinced that her grades were plummeting and that she would be kicked out of the program. But her fears were never realized. Her grades ended up looking very similar to when she was driven by her perfectionism.

OVERGENERALIZATION

With overgeneralization, you take one data point and make a global statement about your person or life, as if this one event speaks to "the way things are." A client with a driving phobia feared having a panic attack and passing out while driving on the freeway. After two months of treatment, he was back on the road with only mild anxiety symptoms. Once in a while, however, the anxiety flared up. It wasn't debilitating anxiety, but it was unpleasant, beyond what he found acceptable. He was still able to drive and successfully manage the episode by using the tools he learned in therapy. But when reporting on such experiences, he would make statements like "I'll never be able to drive without panicking." The recent anxious event not only became exaggerated in his mind but also spoke to a concrete fate that could not be changed. He thought to himself, *I am doomed to be a highly anxious person.* This thought understandably impacted his mood. If this truly were his fate—a future imprisoned by anxiety—a deep sense of loss and a depressed mood would be expected. But this thought didn't actually reflect reality. There were many occasions when he wasn't overwhelmed by anxiety. And when he did feel anxious, he had the understanding and tools to handle the challenge in a healthy way. He realized that through the process of overgeneralization he was unnecessarily spoiling his mood by investing in a narrative that didn't accurately represent his lived experience. He needed to work on seeing and holding on to the successes and the other data points that did not conform to his negative view, which is closely related to the next cognitive distortion.

CONFIRMATION BIAS

With confirmation bias, people see what they want to see. Their mind develops a selective filter, both seeking out data that supports their bias and screening out data that doesn't. A successful female executive I worked with grew up in a family where she was regularly "brought down to size." Because of her parents' own immaturity and woundedness, my client was never allowed to be appropriately big in the world. It was never okay for her to be in the spotlight or celebrated. Instead, they experienced her many academic and athletic achievements as a potential threat. Her gain was experienced as her parents' loss. In the guise of not wanting her to have a "big head," they made sarcastic remarks, withdrew from her, and shifted their attention to the younger siblings. As a result, the client internalized a powerful belief: *Whenever something good happens to me, I'll get knocked down to size.* So, when something good did happen, she automatically felt tense and on guard, expecting things to fall apart at any moment. In an attempt to relieve the unbearable anticipation of the forthcoming attack, whose timing and source she often couldn't predict, she was prone to acting in ways that elicited the punishment or downfall she was expecting, to "get it over with."

Part of our work together was dismantling this cognitive bias that skipped over the positive aspects of her life and latched onto those experiences that fit her negative outlook. When this type of thinking started, it was conceptualized within the framework of TSM. She spotted the cognitive distortion, made an empowering self-statement—*I'm done being afraid; no one can stop me from pursuing my dreams and celebrating my successes*—and redirected her attention and life energy to the front screen.

JUMPING TO CONCLUSIONS/MIND READING

Suppose you walk down the street in your neighborhood. On the other side of the street you see a friend walking toward you. As he approaches, you say hello but he doesn't respond. Your friend keeps his head down and keeps walking. What conclusions do you draw from your friend's behavior? If you lined up ten people who had gone through a similar encounter, you would get a wide range of interpretations. Some would say, "He doesn't want to be my friend anymore" or "He must be mad at me." For others it might be something about the friend's personality: "I always knew he was a jerk." Other interpretations might be that he didn't hear the greeting or is preoccupied with recent news and was not in a frame of mind to interact. The possibilities are limitless.

The takeaway here is that many of the events we experience are blank slates onto which we project our fears and personal conclusions about our self and the world. The depressive side screen will often show negative interpretations. Resist them. Ask yourself, *What other possible interpretations might there be?*

EMOTIONAL REASONING

"I feel like a bad person." One hallmark of childhood trauma, whether it be physical or emotional, is the sense that at your core you are a bad or "toxic" person. It's almost as if the child absorbs the badness of the environment into her person. It helps explain to the young mind why she is being punished. *I am being treated this way because I am bad.* When she leaves the neglectful or abusive home, she doesn't leave behind that feeling of being inherently bad. She carries it into the workplace. She carries it into every significant relationship. To some degree, the feeling of being a bad person always lurks in the background. And with it comes a fear that if others get too close they will run into this unlovable part of herself and reject her, so even her closest relationships are kept at a safe distance. In addition, because she is "bad" she is not worthy of good things. And sometimes it goes further: she feels deserving of bad things and punishment and may allow herself to be mistreated because it fits with her self-perception.

This is but one example of emotional reasoning, whereby the internal perception and emotion become an external reality. Feeling becomes reality and so becomes your fate. All of the side screens we've reviewed will generate different feelings inside you. But you need to remember that a feeling is just a feeling. Your emotional experience doesn't necessarily indicate reality. The thoughts and related feelings generated by the depressive side screen cannot be trusted. Much of the time, your feelings about yourself or your life are the opposite of what's true. As I write this, for example, I'm thinking about the clients in my practice who feel that their very essence is "bad." Every person coming to mind, without exception, is loving and kind. They're *good* people. Others who know them would be shocked to learn that they carry feelings of being a bad person because it's so far from the truth. Watch out for this cognitive distortion.

PERSONALIZATION

Frequently, at the core of depression, is the overwhelming sense of being a failure. Part of what feeds this belief is assuming too much responsibility for the things that go wrong. We refer to this as *personalization*, whereby negative events are connected back to the self. Either you're directly responsible or the universe has your number and is out to get you. If your spouse is in a bad mood, it must be because of something you did. On a weekend getaway, if your friends are not having a thrilling experience, it's your fault. If the family dog develops a medical condition, you're responsible because you could have exercised the dog more and been more vigilant about his health. Or sometimes it's less about responsibility and more about being singled out. You feel like life just treats you differently from other people. If your car breaks down, you throw your hands up in the air: *Why does this kind of thing always happen to me?*

This cognitive distortion, when taken to the extreme, can veer into the realm of magical thinking or a kind of negative omnipotence, whereby one's private, internal experience is the cause of or connected to misfortune. One therapy client felt responsible for the death of his aunt because in an angry moment at the age of ten he had the fleeting thought *I wish she were dead.* Months later, when the aunt died, he felt responsible—that somehow his angry, impulsive thought had caused her death. It was a secret and a burden he'd carried for close to thirty years.

Identifying Your Own Distortions

If you struggle with mood issues and an overactive depressive side screen, it's important to monitor your thought patterns. In particular, you want to watch out for those faulty beliefs and negative patterns that reveal the depressive side screen's presence. Take a moment and review the cognitive distortions we've covered: all-or-nothing thinking, overgeneralization, confirmation bias, jumping to conclusions, emotional reasoning, and personalization. For each one, ask yourself, *Do I tend to think this way?* Maybe one of the illustrations you read in the previous section resonated with your experience. For each cognitive distortion you identify with, try to write down, on a separate piece of paper or on the worksheet at http://www.newharbinger.com/42327, the specific thoughts that show up on the side screen. If it's personalization, for example, maybe a frequent thought is *She isn't paying much attention to me, so she must not like me.* Or maybe you tend to jump to conclusions, especially behind the wheel. When someone cuts in front of you, you automatically think, *The world is filled with jerks!* Write down this thought and others that describe the specific content scrolling across your depressive side screen, related to that cognitive distortion.

Once you've gone through this process, be on the lookout. Expanding on the road rage illustration, as soon as the thought

The world is filled with jerks! comes into your mind, hit the pause button. You're about to invest in the depressive side screen and energize a negative mood by jumping to conclusions. You don't actually know who that driver is. Maybe he's rushing to the hospital or an important school function for his son or daughter. Or maybe he's just a bad driver, which doesn't automatically make him a bad person. Try to apply this approach to the cognitive distortions you've identified.

Anchoring Your Mind to the Front Screen

So far in this chapter, we've been focused on striking a healthy relationship with the depressive side screen—the first step of TSM. We've emphasized raising your awareness and giving you a strategy to detect its presence, one of the primary challenges with this side screen. As soon as you start engaging in the familiar thoughts—exemplifying one or more of the cognitive distortions—you catch yourself and redirect your mind away from that particular thought channel on the depressive side screen.

Now we turn to the second step of TSM, which is moving toward and staying tethered to the front screen. Once you find yourself attending to the depressive side screen, you need to take action. To keep your mind safe from the depressive content, it's important to rotate your attention outward (*get out of your head*) and actively engage in life (*get moving*). In the following section, we'll see how Josh, a client struggling with depressive symptoms, accomplishes these tasks by using the front screen anchors.

Get Out of Your Head and Get Moving

Josh runs to the car, locks the doors, and buries his head into the seat. He hopes no one will come looking for him. A few moments later his parents and older sister are rapping on the car window. He doesn't move. He just wants the world to go away. Eventually he unlocks the doors, but he has no response to the ensuing questions.

At the time of this event, Josh was eight. His family had forced him to join a Little League baseball team. He hated baseball. He was uncoordinated and didn't have any friends on the team. Nothing felt worse than stepping up to plate with the whole world watching and then striking out. He could hear his teammates sigh. He could see the disappointment on the faces around him. The thought of going through it again was unbearable. So, on this particular day, right before the game started, he ran away. He didn't care what people thought or the consequences. He wanted to get away, so he sprinted to the nearest place of refuge—the family car. He slammed the door shut and dreamed of being invisible.

This was not the only time that Josh struggled while growing up. This event was symptomatic of a greater problem. Josh was raised in a cold, emotionally abusive home where he felt as if he could do nothing right. This unloving family environment, combined with the bullying and teasing he got at school for being an awkward kid, made for a difficult childhood. Nothing felt good. At least nothing felt good "out there" in the external world. Josh, like many children in this situation, developed ways of coping with the pain. His most effective strategy was retreating into fantasy. He learned to go away in his mind, a place where no one could hurt him.

Through the various stages of school Josh managed the best he could. He was smart and applied himself enough to gain admittance to a well-regarded university, where he studied finance. While his academic life progressed, his social life and maturity stagnated. He had some acquaintances, but no real friends, at least no one who really knew him. And he preferred it that way, because people didn't feel safe. He didn't have an internal model for relationships feeling good or meeting his needs. Instead, relationships were something to manage, something from which to protect himself.

Despite this protective stance, in college he did cross paths with a persistent woman who practically demanded that they start dating. Interestingly enough, the woman's behavior didn't register as out of line because it was familiar. She could have been his mother. Josh was used to being overpowered by others and going with the flow, while preserving his individuality and finding sanctuary on a psychological island. While he felt compelled to follow the demands of others, he could always go away in his mind; at least there he felt safe and could be left alone. So with no resistance on his part, they started dating and married a year later. She turned out to be an abusive alcoholic. After years of conflict and upheaval, and a few domestic disturbance visits from local police, they finally divorced.

When Josh came to see me at the age of forty-five, he had a diagnosis of major depression, which was being treated pharma-cologically. The antidepressant helped. He was holding down a job at an accounting firm and keeping up with his responsibilities. He felt significantly less depressed and was functioning at a fairly high level.

As good as these results were, however, neither Josh nor his psychiatrist felt the medication was enough. For the most part, his mood was stable during the week, but weekends continued to be a struggle. As soon as he left the office on Friday afternoon, the depression started creeping back in. Sometimes the symptoms became so severe that he had thoughts of ending his life—disappearing for good. Concerned by these thoughts and desper-ate to get relief from the weekend experience, he came in for treatment.

Josh's case is not an aberration. I have worked with several people whose depression follows a similar pattern. During the week they are active and distracted by work and other responsi-bilities. They may not indicate "happy" on a mood scale, depending on the events of the day, but they would deny being out-and-out "depressed." Then Friday rolls around and their mood begins to shift. They no longer have the distraction of work. And if they live alone, which Josh did, they don't have the healthy distraction of close proximal relationships either. Free of demands on their attention, they begin to mentally drift. They go away in their minds and start energizing a negative mood. They take a seat in front of the depressive side screen and begin watching.

At first there is only a small downtick in mood. But the longer the person sits there, the more his mind is flooded with negative messages. His mood becomes more depressed. And the worse he feels, the more the depressing content filling his mind makes sense and rings true. As this cycle escalates, the person is vulnerable to a depressive spiral in which the mood plummets and all feels dark and hopeless. The individual may have been in a stable, hopeful place just a few hours before, but now his perspective on reality has changed. The mind has been saturated with depressive side screen content.

What needs to happen to break this cycle? The first issue Josh and I addressed is similar to the process you went through earlier in the chapter. We identified his cognitive distortions, so he could recognize when he's watching and energizing the side screen. He identified confirmation bias, emotional reasoning, and personalization as the main contributors to his depressive thinking style. This fit with his history. Josh had developed a narrative: the world was a cold, critical place in which he didn't fit or find acceptance. The world around him, and the people populating it, had nothing good to offer him—he was on his own. When he got into his car on a Friday afternoon, with the open space of the weekend before him, he started experiencing the feelings related to his narrative (emotional reasoning). And because he felt alone and rejected by the world around him, he assumed that it must be him—that he was deeply broken or flawed in some way (personalization). As the weekend progressed, every negative experience or perceived failure, such as walking into a messy apartment or remembering calls he hadn't returned, was evidence for his inadequacy and brokenness (confirmation bias).

With this information, Josh began monitoring his thoughts, especially on the weekends. He developed the habit of asking himself several times per day, *Where is my mind right now?* This intervention helped protect him from watching the side screen and was a helpful reminder to use the Mindfulness Skills anchor you read about in chapter 4. He began to recognize the importance of redirecting his attention to the external world and the present moment—a safe distance from the depressive side screen waiting in the recesses of his mind.

Sometimes the intention alone was enough to bring his mind into the present moment. Other times he required more effort to stay on the front screen. He would engage in a household task, such as cleaning the kitchen or vacuuming the floor, or go for a walk with the goal of applying mindfulness principles. For a specified period of time, maybe fifteen or twenty minutes, he would use his five senses to explore and be present with the activity. And Josh's experience and cultivation of mindfulness was further supported by some general mindfulness training. He quickly became a fan of the mindfulness app Headspace. Throughout the week he found pockets of time to listen to one of the guided meditations. With time, as Josh practiced these strategies, he found it easier to rotate his attention outward when he felt vulnerable and drawn to the depressive side screen.

In addition to using the mindfulness anchor, Josh relied on the Healthy Distractions and Activities (HDA) anchor to protect his mood on the weekends. He went through a process very similar to what you did in chapter 6, identifying different kinds of activities that would both meet a healthy need and keep his attention off the depressive side screen. The key for Josh, and for many others when applying this anchor, was to not set the bar too high, scheduling activities that were overly ambitious; if he wasn't able to complete those activities, it would provide evidence for the very cognitive distortions he was trying to change. Instead of making a plan to swim fifty laps (*physical activity*) at the local YMCA on Saturday, for example, he started with a brisk walk around his neighborhood. For *enlivening activities*, he took small steps toward increased aliveness. He loved researching interesting people and ideas, so he would read about a *challenging* but interesting topic online or go to his local bookstore (*adventure*) and browse the biographical section. He also tried to incorporate some social activities into his weekend schedule. After a gap of many years, he began attending Sunday services at his local church and started looking into various groups and activities offered there. For Josh, the HDA anchor took the form of a well-thought-out weekend plan that he followed closely. It offered a safe home for his mind and lifted his sense of well-being in the process.

Conclusion

In this chapter, we explored the depressive side screen—how it shows up in your internal world, the way it captures your attention, and how you can respond to protect your emotional well-being.

One major focus of the chapter was on understanding and identifying the types of thoughts that are common to the depressive side screen. You were introduced to six cognitive distortions: all-or-nothing thinking, overgeneralization, confirmation bias, jumping to conclusions, emotional reasoning, and personalization. When you find yourself engaging in this type of thinking, it functions as an early detection system, alerting you to the presence of the side screen.

Then, in the final section of the chapter, you were taken through a case example where the two steps of TSM were applied. You observed Josh striking a healthy relationship with his depressive side screen by identifying his cognitive distortions and monitoring his thought life and you also observed him applying the Mindfulness Skills and HDA anchors to stay active and more attuned to the present moment—activities that kept his mind off the side screen and moved his life forward in a positive way.

In the next chapter, we'll explore the third and final front screen anchor you can use to apply TSM, Loving Action. As you'll see, the Loving Action anchor turns side screen activity—whether it's on the anxious, addictive, or depressive side screen—into an opportunity to be a loving influence. The very thoughts and feelings that have been a source of pain become a reminder and natural catalyst to put your attention and concern on others. Let's see how it works.

CHAPTER 8

LOVING ACTION ANCHOR
Using the Side Screen for Good

A few years ago, I worked with a woman in her sixties who struggled with separation anxiety—intense fears related to being apart from loved ones. A primary focus of treatment was preparing her for an upcoming trip. Her daughter had just given birth to a second child, and my client was desperate to lay eyes on her new grandbaby. The challenge was that my client's daughter lived on the opposite coast, and no one was available to take the trip with my client. Her husband was overseas on business, and other family members were tied down with work and parental responsibilities. But before she could talk herself out of it, the client booked the flight and contacted me to address the ensuing anxiety.

From the beginning of treatment, the client's personality shone brightly. She was a warm, vivacious woman who naturally encouraged others. It was her trademark. She was known as the bright light who lifted people's spirits. You couldn't help but smile and feel good in her presence. Unfortunately, it was this very part of herself—the part that was a blessing to others and a personal source of joy—that the anxiety squelched. When she was caught up in a cycle of anxious worry, she found it difficult to be the person she wanted to be. The bright light faded as she clammed up and turned her attention and concern inward.

In her preparation for the upcoming trip, we wondered how she might tap into and leverage her gift of encouragement. Introducing this possibility created an immediate shift in her demeanor. Her tone of voice changed from apprehension to playfulness, as she entertained what encouragement might look like on her trip to the East Coast. The idea of transforming an anxious event—traveling by herself—into an opportunity to encourage others was a welcome paradigm shift.

As the day of the trip approached, she had a plan. Regardless of how she was feeling, she had a focus and a heartfelt mission. Instead of ruminating on the fearful thoughts scrolling across the side screen, she was determined to use the anxious energy for positive action—to be an encourager.

She found plenty of opportunities. She thanked the ticket agent for her professionalism and helpfulness. On the escalator, she complimented a woman on her outfit. While going through security, she thanked a TSA agent for his patience and sense of humor. Winding her way through the airport toward her gate, she left a wake of warm feelings and lifted spirits—a disposition she carried throughout the trip. Instead of allowing the anxiety to stifle her personality, she used the side screen energy to express the best of who she was.

What Is the Loving Action Anchor?

This woman's story is a good illustration of making use of the Loving Action anchor—the third front screen anchor. You take your current challenge—the anxious feeling, the negative mood—and turn it into an opportunity to positively influence the lives of others. Instead of turning inward and focusing on yourself when you feel afraid or overwhelmed, you use the Loving Action anchor to stay outwardly focused, directing your concern to the well-being of others. And when you engage in loving action in the midst of your anxious experience, you disrupt the old pattern of allowing your feelings to dictate what you will or won't do—and you feel the contentment that comes with expressing the best of who you are.

In this chapter, you will learn how to use the Loving Action anchor in two primary ways. First, you will see how you can use side screen activity as a natural reminder and springboard toward expressing loving behavior. As you will discover, you can convert the same anxious feelings and worries that have held you back from fully living into a natural ally for positive action. After you learn this process of converting side screen energy into virtuous behavior, we'll focus on the second way you can use this front screen anchor: to increase loving action in your life, irrespective of what's happening on the side screen. You don't need to wait around for worries or unhealthy urges to announce themselves (side screen activity) before you start moving your life forward in a meaningful way. You can be proactive and put a structure in place that helps you cultivate and express the person you want to be.

Defining Loving Action

You may have questions about the type of love we're referring to with the Loving Action anchor. *Love* is a loaded word with all sorts of meanings. It can be an expression of romantic passion ("I'm madly in love with you!"), or the deep commitment and care you have for a family member or close friend, or even your affinity for a particular activity—"I love to play tennis!"

The ancient Greeks actually had separate words for these various expressions of love. Their term for erotic love, *eros*, denoted the sexual passion and all-consuming infatuation that young lovers experience. Then there was *philia*—friendship love—and a type of love referred to as *pragma*, the love experienced in a long-term committed relationship, requiring compromise, patience, and mutual support. They even had a word for self-love, *philautia*, which could be expressed in either a positive way, such as having healthy self-esteem, or a negative way, for the person who was narcissistic and felt superior to others. And then there was *agape*, a selfless form of love not motivated by a feeling or self-interest—an expression of love meant to serve and benefit the lives of others.

For the purposes of this chapter, love is broadly defined as any action intended for the good or well-being of others. It's the kind of love the ancient Greeks would call philia, pragma, or agape—especially agape. The Loving Action anchor is best thought of as a vehicle to express agape love, whereby you transform a vulnerable moment—a time when you're prone to anxious preoccupation and self-focus—into an act of kindness or some other action that positively affects another person's life. Let's see how it works.

Converting Side Screen Activity into Loving Action

When you worry, feel down, or cope in unhealthy ways, there is usually a cost. You may find it hard to listen or be fully present in your important relationships. Maybe you stay home or stop communicating with people you care about. Whatever it may be, in the midst of your struggle there is usually a loss. You're not able to fully enjoy life or be the person you want to be, which can be an additional source of emotional pain. On top of your anxious struggle or negative mood is a second layer of suffering: the painful awareness of missing out—of not fully living. You feel the emotional consequences of being shut down as a person and blocked from the life you want.

The Loving Action anchor addresses this problem by shaking up the stimulus-response pattern in which you're currently stuck. In the present context, the *stimulus* is the side screen activity—the worries, the urges, the anxious feelings—all of the problematic thoughts and feelings showing up in your internal world. The *response* is what you do in the face of this side screen activity—the internal and external actions you take that energize the destructive inner activity and constrict you as a person.

In the following section, you will be guided through a process of replacing this damaging stimulus-response pattern—with the resulting pain and problems in your life—with a new life-giving pattern. Using a three-step process, you will create a new stimulus-response pattern that turns your side screen (stimulus) into an automatic reminder and catalyst for virtuous action (new response). The process begins by first identifying those parts of you most negatively impacted by the side screen. You will discover how to activate and leverage these when the internal challenge (side screen) arises.

Step One: Counting the Cost

Table 8.1 presents twenty-one words that represent loving actions. To get the action part, imagine placing *the act of* in front of each term—*the act of* patience, *the act of* generosity, and so on. In a moment I'll ask you to complete the Compromised Loving Action exercise; in it, you'll identify those loving actions from the table that tend to get shut down and lost when you worry or feel emotionally overwhelmed.

Table 8.1. Loving Actions

Patience	Humor	Self-Control
Compassion	Creativity	Generosity
Kindness	Encouragement	Understanding
Service	Forgiveness	Humility
Gratitude	Spirituality	Affection
Honesty	Courage	Curiosity
Attentiveness	Optimism	Availability

As you go through the terms, don't worry about how each word is defined. What's important is the meaning of the act of *service* or *compassion* to *you*. The table is merely a tool to help you examine, in a nuanced way, the cost of your current struggle. You may even want to include loving actions not listed or change the wording of a term to better reflect your experience. Your only task—and the key to the exercise—is evaluating the terms through the lens of your impact on others and the world around you. You're trying to assess how your current struggle has interfered with being a positive, loving influence on others. For those few terms in the table that seem more individualistic and less obviously an act of love, try to find the relational connection. Creativity, for example, could mean redesigning your child's bedroom or helping a friend find a creative solution to a problem. Taking a couple of deep breaths (self-control) in the presence of a loved one, instead of blowing up out of frustration, could also be an expression of love. The same is true of reminding yourself to stay open and receive information being shared by a colleague at work (humility).

COMPROMISED LOVING ACTION EXERCISE

For this exercise, you're thinking about the outward expression or relational impact of each term in table 8.1. To begin the exercise, reflect on your struggle—the issue you want to change. What happens when you feel anxious? What happens when you're stuck in a bad mood or preoccupied with fulfilling an unhealthy desire? In the midst of these experiences, what do you tend to do or not do, and how are others impacted by your typical response pattern? What positive expressions of self are silenced? With these types of questions as the backdrop, thoughtfully and systematically go through each word in the table. Beginning with patience, ask yourself, *Do I lose patience with others when I feel anxious or feel down?* If so, circle the word. Then go to the next loving action.

What happens to compassion when I'm struggling? Does my capacity for caring (compassion) stay the same or is it suppressed? If the latter is true, circle it. Go through table 8.1 in this fashion, circling the loving actions that tend to get stifled when your side screen is fully active. It doesn't matter how many you circle. If you feel the loving behavior is compromised, circle it. Take a few minutes to complete this step of the exercise.

Once you've reviewed all the terms, step back and take note of the words you've circled. These circles represent the footprint that worry and anxiety have left on your life—the ways the side screen has blocked you from being fully alive and expressing the best parts of who you are. The intention here is not to dwell on the negative. You already know there is a cost to your struggle—you feel it. Rather, the goal is to use this detailed inventory—assessing the cost—as a way to promote positive change in your life. In a moment, you'll work on systematically expressing the loving actions you've just circled in the midst of challenging emotional experiences. But before we move on to this step of turning your list into a powerful tool for change, we need to do a little trimming. It's hard to change everything at once. As you begin implementing the Loving Action anchor, you'll want to focus on those loving behaviors that are most important to you and most deeply impacted—in a negative way—by your current struggle.

So, let's identify your top four most compromised loving actions. Review the loving actions you circled in table 8.1. Which are most important to you? Which generate the greatest sense of loss when they're absent from your life? Which most directly impact your relationships? With these questions in mind, begin paring down your list, crossing off those loving actions that are relatively less significant in terms of either their relative importance to you or the degree to which they're compromised. Once you've narrowed the list down to four loving actions, write them in the left-hand column in table 8.2. (You can download a worksheet for this exercise at http://www.newharbinger.com/42327.) We'll get back to the right-hand column shortly.

Table 8.2. My Four Loving Actions

Compromised Loving Actions	Positive Loving Actions

Step Two: Defining What Love Looks Like

Now that you've identified the expressions of love most compromised by your current struggle, you're ready for the next step, in which you flip the script and begin the process of taking a negative in your life and turning it into a positive. It starts with you describing—in positive terms—what each of the four loving actions in table 8.2 looks like. In other words, what are you doing, in concrete behavioral terms, when you express these virtues? What would a fly on the wall see you doing or hear you saying when fully expressing these traits? For example, my client in the chapter opener, who faced travel alone, translated encouragement into the following action steps:

- Observe positive traits in others and express it: "You have a great sense of humor."

- Notice challenging circumstances and offer verbal support: "Thanks for being so patient" (to the TSA worker at the airport).

- Compliment others on their appearance: "I love your dress."

Following this model, try to describe your four positive loving actions (right-hand column of table 8.2) in concrete, actionable terms. What are the behaviors or verbal expressions that represent *generosity* or *optimism* or *affection* in your life? Write your answers in the table's right-hand column. Ideally, you want to come up with at least two specific deeds for each of the four loving actions. The emphasis is on being a positive influence in the lives of others, but don't feel overly constricted by these guidelines. Write down what comes to mind; you can always make changes later. Also, keep in mind that you can express love in small, subtle ways. Sharing an authentic feeling (*honesty*) or holding the door for someone (*service* or *kindness*) can—at least for our purposes—be a loving action. Take a few minutes to complete My Four Loving Actions.

Step Three: Associating Loving Behavior with Side Screen Activity

The third step is creating a natural association between side screen activity and loving action by repeatedly engaging in loving behaviors in the presence of anxious thoughts and feelings. This is where you'll create a new stimulus-response pattern. Instead of watching the side screen or pulling away from others or turning your attention to yourself when you feel anxious and worried, you act on one of the behaviors you described in the Positive Loving Actions column of My Four Loving Actions. You begin the practice of pairing side screen activation with positive, loving action. As you consistently introduce loving behaviors in the face of side screen activation, you create a new association—a new reflex. The anxious feeling—the worrisome thought and the potentially destructive urge—become an automatic reminder to live out one of your values. You'll use the energy being generated by the challenging feeling and other side screen activity as a tailwind to express the best parts of who you are.

Let's turn to some examples to see how this works.

A working mother with two children in middle school wanted to address her drinking habit. At the end of her workday, the first thing she did when arriving home was open up a bottle of chilled white wine. Drinking helped her relax and get through the final push of making dinner, helping kids with homework, going through their bedtime routine, cleaning the kitchen, and so on.

Part of her treatment involved completing the Compromised Loving Action exercise (table 8.1). She went through the list of twenty-one loving actions, circling those expressions of love that were suppressed or compromised by her drinking. She circled ten loving actions. From the list of ten, she then identified the four loving behaviors she believed to be the most negatively impacted by the habit. She was most aware of how alcohol negatively impacted her relationship with her husband and kids. After the second glass of wine, she became less attentive (*attentiveness*) and more detached (*availability*) from these important relationships. Even though family was her highest priority, the wine blunted her awareness and conscious concern (*compassion*) for those she loved most. Even when she felt the disconnect and tried to self-correct, it was often too late. The kids were less interested in connecting when they spotted "Mom's glassy-eyed look." And her husband, sensing her lack of availability earlier in the evening, had already moved on to his own personal interests, whether that was tinkering in the garage or watching a TV program. Lastly, the drinking habit impeded her spiritual growth (*spirituality*). Faith and feeling connected to God was an important resource and source of meaning for this client. When she neglected this part of herself, she suffered from a sense of emptiness and lack of purpose. One of the main ways she fed her spiritual life was through reading inspirational and faith-based books. But after two or three glasses of wine, she either wasn't in the mood to read or could only get through a couple pages before nodding off.

After identifying her top four most compromised loving actions (*attentiveness*, *compassion*, *availability*, and *spirituality*), she went through each one describing ways she could live out this important value. That is, she described what *attentiveness* or *compassion* looked like when she was at her best—when she stayed true to the best version of herself. She came up with concrete ways of expressing each loving action, which are presented in table 8.3.

Table 8.3. My First Client's Four Loving Actions

Compromised Loving Action	Positive Loving Actions
Attentiveness	Asking the kids about their day and offering them her undivided attention; rubbing her husband's shoulders, where he tends to hold stress; taking a moment to think through what the kids will need for tomorrow, whether it be clean articles of clothing or items for their lunch.
Compassion	Saying "I love you"; internally reflecting on her husband's current life stressors; inquiring about an issue that has been troubling a loved one, such as a friendship at school or a work challenge.
Availability	Asking her husband if he wants to go for a walk after dinner; letting the kids know she's available to help with homework if needed; pausing and mentally reminding herself to stay relationally open and engaged.
Spirituality	Saying grace at the dinner table; reminding herself of the things she's grateful for in life; read a spiritually based book for thirty minutes before bedtime.

By filling in the table, she created a well-defined list of loving actions she could use in the change process. These loving behaviors (right-hand column) became her new response(s) to the challenging stimulus—her urge to cope and self-soothe with drinking. Up to this point she had been stuck in a negative stimulus-response pattern. When the addictive side screen lit up, she felt the urge to drink (stimulus) and automatically poured herself a glass of wine (response). Now, equipped with her list of loving actions, she started interrupting the pattern. In the face of temptation, she looked over her list and acted on one or more of the loving behaviors. She asked the kids about their day. The addictive side screen served as a reminder to connect with her husband and see if he wanted to take a walk, as well as with her desire to have some quiet time to feed her spiritual life. As she set her mind to this practice, engaging in loving action when she felt like drinking, over the subsequent days and weeks a new stimulus-response pattern was created. The very stimulus that used to trigger the unhealthy behavior of mindless drinking was converted into a positive. The urge for white wine became a natural reminder and energy source for expressing loving behavior.

Before you start developing a new stimulus-response pattern with the Loving Action anchor, let's make sure this process of converting side screen activity into loving action is crystal clear. Let's turn to an illustration where anxiety is the primary issue.

A screenwriter in the film industry came to see me for obsessive anxiety. All of her anxious worries, which varied in specifics from day to day, tended to coalesce around one central theme. She was deathly afraid of failing or "screwing up," on both a job-performance level and a moral or character level. With respect to the latter, there were times when she feared that she had inadvertently broken a law or had been immoral in some way. She could spend hours reviewing in her mind possible misstatements made on her tax return. Catching herself exceeding the speed limit triggered an irrational—but powerful—fear of being thrown into jail. And then there were the job-related fears—anxious worries that frequently targeted her writing. Even though she was a gifted writer, producing a script could be a painful process riddled with obsessive worrying and paralyzing perfectionism. At times she got stuck in a space where nothing seemed good enough. She would write and rewrite the same sentences over and over again. As deadlines approached, her anxiety could reach near-panic levels, and it was all she could do not to "lose it."

In going through the Compromised Loving Action exercise (table 8.1) she identified *humor, creativity, kindness*, and *gratitude* as her top four most compromised loving behaviors when the anxiety took over. Then she wrote out specific behavioral expressions for each of the loving actions. Table 8.4 shows what she wrote down.

Table 8.4. My Second Client's Four Loving Actions

Compromised Loving Action	Positive Loving Action
Humor	Tell jokes; create levity and laughter with humorous comments and interpretations of fears and unwelcome life events.
Creativity	Spruce up the office environment with flowers, a new fragrance, and the like; help others with creative problem solving.
Kindness	Make encouraging statements; offer thoughtful gestures and gifts.
Gratitude	Express gratitude to others; be thankful for a satisfying career.

After generating a list of concrete behaviors that expressed her top four loving actions, she was ready to apply the Loving Action anchor. When a worry entered her mind, she looked over her menu of positive behaviors (right-hand column) and took action. When anxious thoughts and feelings arose, she began introducing *humor*. She pulled out her book of jokes and recited a few to a writing colleague. She experimented with humorously exaggerating, in her own mind, the perceived concern. On one occasion she passed a highway patrol car, which triggered her obsession about being pulled over. With her husband in the car, she leveraged her storytelling skills and expanded on the fearful narrative. She described being followed by the CIA and FBI and how she was the world's most wanted fugitive for not using her car blinker appropriately. She took the fear to such a ridiculous point that both she and her husband erupted in laughter. It even provided some healthy reality testing, allowing her to see the worry from a more balanced perspective.

She also found ways to express her *creativity*. Instead of going away in her mind and worrying about the upcoming deadline, she burned a pleasing incense and placed a beautiful bouquet of flowers in the middle of the writers' room. She even used side screen activity as an opportunity for creative problem solving, whether that was helping a writer with character development or a story arc or brainstorming with a friend or family member who needed to make an important decision.

This client also found ways to express more *kindness* and *gratitude*. When she was on set, the presence of the anxious side screen became a reminder to say a kind word or grab a cup of coffee for a member of the crew. Worries and anxious feelings were also paired with acts of gratitude. She paused and reflected on the relationships for which she was grateful. Then she would express this verbally or send a quick text: "Just wanted you to know that I appreciate you and our friendship." In short, she used the Loving Action anchor to systematically associate worry and anxiety with thoughtful and appreciative behavior.

Now it's your turn to apply the Loving Action anchor. When the side screen lights up and the anxious worry grabs your attention, you want to accept the hard feeling, while channeling your attention and life energy into a loving action. Make the firm commitment to be a blessing to others. Even though the pull is to rotate your attention inward and look for a way to reestablish a sense of emotional security, make the courageous and value-based decision to place your loving concern on others. Review your list of potential positive behaviors from your Four Loving Actions (table 8.2) and take action. Identify the loving action that seems most accessible and applicable for the situation you're in and express it without delay. Engage in an act of *kindness*. Call a friend who's been wanting to talk (*availability*). Pray for someone in need (*compassion* and *spirituality*).

As you continue this practice of consistently responding to internal challenges with loving action, a new set of behaviors will become automatically paired with your side screen. The presence of worries and anxious feelings—and other side screen challenges—will become reflexive reminders and catalysts for virtuous behavior. You will experience the satisfaction of converting your side screen—a historical source of pain—into a springboard for helping others and being your best.

Loving Action as a Way of Life

So far in this chapter, you've been using loving action in response to side screen activity, whereby the anxious feeling or unhealthy temptation becomes a reminder to do the very thing—positive action—that normally gets lost. When you associate loving action with the internal challenge, you disrupt the old stimulus-response pattern. Instead of the destructive mood or worrisome thought causing you to compromise what you care about in life, which is your old pattern, you use the side screen as an internal reminder and energy source to express the best parts of who you are. This is deeply satisfying.

Now we shift to the second way you can apply the Loving Action anchor. Instead of focusing on how you react to internal challenges, in this section we're more interested in who you want to be, regardless of what is happening on the side screen. Your pursuit of loving action is independent from your worry and anxiety. It's about identifying the parts of yourself you want to grow and putting a structure in place to support this character development.

This process begins by identifying the parts of yourself you most want to nurture.

Loving Actions Close to Your Heart

If your experience mirrors mine, you've had many thoughts about what needs to change in your life or the ways in which you'd like to grow. You read an article, listen to a motivating speaker, or have a personal experience that inspires you to make a change. Some of these change efforts, spurred on by these various influences, stick and are sustained over time, while others—maybe the majority—fall by the wayside. When our personal growth efforts are unsuccessful, it's often for one of two reasons. First, it could be the articulated goal doesn't line up with both your head and your heart. Eating a meatless diet may sound good—you believe in it and see its value—but, for whatever reason, it may stay primarily in the theoretical realm and not translate into actual practice. You don't *feel* its importance. The aspirational idea doesn't penetrate to your heart, where you would find the internal energy and motivation to carry out the new behavior. With no organic feelings supporting the good idea, the desired new behavior—whether it's being more grateful or more honest or more compassionate—either is never realized or quickly fades from your life.

A second potential barrier to successful change is the absence of a structure that supports the new set of behaviors. You may put a high value on a healthy diet and exercise—and even feel it on a heart level—but if you don't create a life structure that offers protected space to work out regularly and do some thoughtful shopping and meal planning, your goals will be eclipsed by competing demands and the busyness of life.

The balance of this chapter is designed to address these two challenges. You will first complete an exercise that helps you identify those loving actions that line up with both your head and your heart. Once you're equipped with this list, we'll explore different ways of supporting the consistent expression of the traits you've identified. The key is putting a system in place that nurtures loving behaviors over time in your busy, distracted life.

THE LOVING ACTION ASSESSMENT

This simple assessment measures the relative importance of the twenty-one loving actions you considered earlier in the chapter. As you take the assessment, try to avoid responding from a place of *should* (*this loving behavior* should *be important to me, so I will rate it highly*) or worrying about how your responses might be perceived by others. This is for your eyes only. Your goal is to evaluate each loving action in terms of how it lines up with your head and your heart, regardless of whether it's currently being expressed in your life. Circle the number that corresponds with the rating you assign each loving action. To the best of your ability, you want to assign the highest ratings to those loving actions that you not only believe in intellectually but also feel on a heart level.

Once you've completed the assessment, look over your responses and write down all the loving actions you rated a 4 (important) or 5 (very important). Depending on how many loving actions fall into these categories, you may want to trim your list down to no more than ten loving actions. A good place to start is removing the loving actions that you're already working on from earlier in the chapter (your top four most compromised loving actions in table 8.2). To continue trimming, maybe you'll write down only those with a 5 rating (very important) or include only some of the loving actions you rated at 4 (important). Feel free to experiment. This is not an exact science. You're trying to create a list that is fully connected with your person—both head and heart—while protecting yourself from being overwhelmed by behaviors you're trying to cultivate. Just keep in mind that it's better to start small and experience some success than it is to take on too much and get discouraged.

Table 8.5. Loving Action Assessment

Rating system:

1 = currently not important; 2 = less important; 3 = somewhat important; 4 = important; 5 = very important

1. Gratitude	1	2	3	4	5
2. Patience	1	2	3	4	5
3. Compassion	1	2	3	4	5
4. Humor	1	2	3	4	5
5. Service	1	2	3	4	5
6. Courage	1	2	3	4	5
7. Forgiveness	1	2	3	4	5
8. Creativity	1	2	3	4	5
9. Spirituality/Faith	1	2	3	4	5
10. Kindness	1	2	3	4	5
11. Availability	1	2	3	4	5
12. Encouragement	1	2	3	4	5
13. Honesty	1	2	3	4	5
14. Generosity	1	2	3	4	5
15. Optimism	1	2	3	4	5
16. Self-Discipline	1	2	3	4	5
17. Humility	1	2	3	4	5
18. Attentiveness	1	2	3	4	5
19. Understanding	1	2	3	4	5
20. Affection	1	2	3	4	5
21. Curiosity	1	2	3	4	5

Once you have your list of approximately ten loving actions, you need to translate each into action steps. This is the same process you went through earlier of describing the outward manifestation of the given loving action—how *generosity*, or *kindness*, or whatever the trait may be, is expressed through behavior in your life. Spend a few minutes defining each of the loving actions on your list. Try to come up with at least two concrete behaviors for each loving action.

Creating a Structure to Support Loving Actions

Around 1730, a young Benjamin Franklin sat down and listed thirteen virtues that he wanted to define his life. He then created a charting system that allowed him to keep track of how he was doing in terms of living up to his virtues. His approach was to focus on one virtue per week. Come evening, he would reflect on his day, trying to recall the occasions when he failed to live out the given virtue. For each shortfall he placed a black dot in the space next to the virtue on his ledger. At the end of the week he moved on to the next virtue. At the end of thirteen weeks, having cycled through all thirteen virtues, he started the process over again. Franklin began this practice as a young man and continued it until his death. He often credited his lifelong commitment to these thirteen virtues as a key to his success. He was quick to state that he could never fully live up to his ideals. What he did notice, however, was a trend. As the years went by there were fewer and fewer black dots next to his virtues.

Benjamin Franklin's approach to change captures the spirit of what we're trying to accomplish. He created a system and set of rituals that kept virtuous behavior in the forefront of his mind and supported sustained personal growth. In the same way, you want to implement a structure into your life that will help you cultivate the loving behaviors you've identified in the Loving Action Assessment (table 8.5). Here's how one client approached the task.

Kevin is a business executive in his mid-forties. He suffers from chronic stress, depressed moods, and persistent worries about uncertain outcomes—*Will the company meet earnings? Will my kids get into a good college? What if I lose my job and I can't pay the bills?* and so on. When he took the Loving Action Assessment, he ended up with twelve loving actions with a rating of 5 (very important), four with a rating of 4 (important), two with a rating of 3 (somewhat important), and two with a rating of 2 (less important).

Similar to the step you completed, Kevin wrote down the twelve loving actions that received a rating of 5. Once he had his list, he crossed off the loving actions he was already working on from earlier in the chapter: *gratitude, compassion, optimism,* and *curiosity.* These were parts of himself that ended up being stifled when he felt stressed and overwhelmed. Once he removed these four from his list, he was left with eight loving actions on which to focus: *service, courage, spirituality, kindness, availability, encouragement, honesty,* and *generosity.*

Now his goal was to put a ritual or system in place that would help him invest in and cultivate these loving behaviors. Kevin decided to take Franklin's weekly theme approach, a model you too may want to follow. In week one Kevin focused on more fully expressing *service.* He set the word *service* as an all-day event for the week on his computer calendar, so he could see the heading and be reminded of his goal throughout each day of the week. Each morning and several times later each day he reminded himself to be of service. Sometimes it was as simple as holding the door open for someone or calling his wife on the way home and asking if she needed anything from the supermarket. Other times this loving action required more thought and effort. He decided to be an extra driver for his daughter's school field trip, and he talked to the director of a local nonprofit about possibly joining the financial committee—an area where others could benefit from his skill set.

Kevin followed this pattern for each of the eight loving action items on his list. Each morning he reviewed his list—along with the concrete actions steps for the trait he wanted to express—and restated the mission: "I want to be an *encourager* today" or "I will do my best to be present and *available* to others today." After eight weeks he decided to cycle through his loving action list a second time; then he gradually started incorporating loving actions that he'd given a 4 rating, such as *patience* and *self-discipline*. Similar to Benjamin Franklin's experience, Kevin didn't always stay true to his daily or weekly goal. There were days when work pressures and other demands caused him to be distracted and drift from the program he had put in place. This was to be expected. But then something would bring his goal back to mind. Maybe it was a quiet moment or seeing the loving action on his calendar or coming across the list from the Loving Action Assessment in his journal that brought his change program back into focus. When this happened, he quickly tried to implement a loving behavior as a way to get back on track and reestablish positive momentum.

Following Kevin's example, you need to put a system in place that will support your list of virtuous behaviors. Maybe each month has a theme for which you focus on one loving action. January is the month when you practice *curiosity* in your relationships, for example; then February is dedicated to *honesty*, and you look for appropriate ways to be more open and authentic in your relationships; and so on. Or maybe, similar to Kevin, you focus on one loving action per week. Alternatively, you could elect to cultivate two or more loving actions at the same time. There is no right or wrong approach. It might even be fun and helpful to invite your spouse or friend into the change process. Have them take the Loving Action Assessment; then both of you can hold each other accountable and provide mutual encouragement. The key is establishing a routine that reminds you of what you're trying to accomplish, holds you accountable, and keeps you motivated.

For additional support, you may want to use other resources, such as the VIA Institute on Character. VIA, which stands for *virtues in action*, is an organization dedicated to helping people identify and develop character strengths, such as perseverance and self-regulation. Although character strengths, as defined by VIA, aren't synonymous with loving actions, there are areas of significant overlap, where working on a particular character trait is the equivalent of expressing a loving behavior (loving action). On their website (http://www.viacharacter.org) you will find helpful exercises and specific recommendations on how you can develop and express virtuous behavior.

Books and workbooks that feature acceptance and commitment therapy (ACT) are another valuable resource. ACT is a treatment approach that places a heavy emphasis on pursuing deeply held values in the presence of feelings that normally hold you back from living a full, meaningful life. In workbooks such as *Get Out of Your Mind and Into Your Life* (Hayes and Smith, 2005) and *The Mindfulness and Acceptance Workbook for Anxiety* (Forsyth and Eifert, 2016) you will find a wide range of exercises designed to support value-based action in your daily life.

Conclusion

In this chapter, you were introduced to the Loving Action anchor. In the first section, you worked on converting side screen energy—the presence of anxious thoughts and feelings—into a natural catalyst for positive action. This process has three main steps. First, you completed the Compromised Loving Action exercise to identify the loving behaviors typically suppressed by your current challenge. In the second step, you examined your top four most compromised values in terms of loving action and described specific ways you could positively live out these values. This process gave you a list of concrete loving behaviors that you could then use to create a new stimulus-response pattern. In the third step, you explored the power of engaging in loving action when challenged by your side screen. By systematically introducing positive, loving action in the presence of your worries or challenging moods, you develop a new automatic response with your side screen. The challenging thoughts and feelings become a natural reminder and energizer for loving, caring behavior.

The second part of the chapter focused on cultivating more loving action in your life regardless of what is happening on the side screen. You learned how you could use the Loving Action anchor for personal growth independent of your worry and anxiety. You took an assessment to rank the relative importance of twenty-one loving actions, followed by recommendations and possible models for consistently increasing the presence of loving behaviors in your life.

Now that you've been introduced to all aspects of TSM—the different types of side screens and all three front screen anchors— it's time to put all the pieces together and see the method applied to a real clinical case.

CHAPTER 9

THE TWO-SCREEN METHOD FULLY APPLIED
The Case of Ms. J

At this point in the book, you're familiar with each aspect of the Two-Screen Method. Beginning with chapter 3 (Freedom from the Anxious Side Screen), you've been actively applying the principle of Accept & Redirect to the challenging thoughts and feelings that show up on your side screen. And along the way, you've been cultivating mindfulness skills (Mindfulness Skills anchor) and learning how to redirect your attention and life energy into positive, healthy action with the HDA and Loving Action anchors.

In this chapter, everything you've learned about TSM is integrated and applied to an actual clinical case that was conducted and filmed in 2012 for educational and training purposes. You'll enter the therapy room and observe as Ms. J, a single thirty-year-old woman with anxiety symptoms, applies TSM over the course of ten weeks. (A note: While Ms. J consented to record her sessions and use them for teaching purposes—including this book—certain aspects of her case, including identifiers that could jeopardize her anonymity, have been modified for confidentiality and teaching objectives.)

The chapter is organized by session, so you can see how and when different aspects of TSM are used. In the early sessions, a lot happens in the therapy room in terms of my involvement and the material covered, for two reasons. First, the book you're holding wasn't available in 2012. Though Ms. J was supplied with some materials, such as exercises for the front screen anchors, most of TSM needed to be communicated verbally in session. After Ms. J had a solid grasp of how the method works, I took on a less active role, and most of her TSM application was done outside the therapy room. Second, in the first several sessions, due to Ms. J's particular anxiety symptoms, I helped her systematically face her fears with exposure therapy—a topic you explored in chapter 3 and hopefully have applied with the Freedom Ladder. While some of the exposure therapy I conducted with Ms. J is fairly complex, and probably best suited for the therapy room, most of the exposure work is straightforward and could be effectively addressed with the resources you've been given (that is, the Freedom Ladder). For the vast majority of the issues addressed in Ms. J's treatment, my involvement could be replaced with the information, tools, and guidance provided in this book.

The Two-Screen Method, supported by the materials you've read, is designed for your independent use and application. While seeking out personal therapy is encouraged—and sometimes needed—TSM doesn't require professional assistance. That's one of its primary benefits. TSM makes it easy to apply mindfulness principles and other helpful psychological strategies in your daily life whether you're in therapy or not.

The First Session

After a quick introduction, we settle into the therapy room and begin exploring Ms. J's anxious experience. Her anxiety appears to express itself in two primary ways, the first being social anxiety. Anticipating social situations and interacting with others generates high levels of anxiety for her. The anxiety is fueled by a general fear of embarrassment and potential humiliation. She fears saying something "stupid" or having her mind go blank when asked a question. She fears being a burden to others or having others experience her as "boring." Because of these fears, she finds it difficult to assert herself in basic ways. She is reluctant to return purchased items, even if the item is damaged or not to her liking. She doesn't speak up in restaurants when there has been a mistake with her order, and she tends to stay quiet when a friend misconstrues something she has said. She stays silent in these situations because she's paralyzed by the possibility of others viewing her negatively.

The second anxious theme is obsessive anxiety, which shows up in two primary ways. First, Ms. J is chronically concerned about contracting a virus or becoming ill. She's hyper-attuned to bodily symptoms and has a narrow range of acceptability for what her body should or shouldn't be experiencing. A skipped heartbeat immediately goes to *I'm having a heart attack!* An upset stomach triggers obsessive worrying about stomach cancer. Her obsessive anxiety also shows up in the form of intrusive violent images. Ms. J. will be walking down the sidewalk and suddenly an image of a fatal car accident will pop into her mind. She knows the images are a product of her own mind, but they're unwanted and highly disturbing, and they seem to come out of nowhere. This type of anxious experience is often seen with obsessive-compulsive disorder, where people are plagued by anxious ideas and images that involuntarily come into awareness. They may recognize the obsessive concern as irrational or unworthy of their attention, but the feeling—the anxious spike they experience— makes it *feel* real and hard to ignore. For our purposes, however, Ms. J's intrusive images, as well as her health fears, fall under the more general category of obsessive anxiety.

On most days, she reports an anxiety level that ranges from 65/100 to 80/100, with 100/100 being the highest level of anxiety and 0/100 reflecting no anxious symptoms. Recently, she's found it overwhelming to just leave the house in the morning and worries about her ability to hold down a job in her current state.

Current Coping Strategies

After getting a profile of her anxious side screen, we explore her common reactions, both mentally and behaviorally, to anxiety. This helps us see the role that the *spotlight of attention* (watching the side screen), *reactivity* (fighting or resisting the anxious feeling), and *avoidance behaviors* (attempts to avoid activating the side screen in the first place) play in her anxious experience.

Ms. J reports a pattern of avoiding known activities or situations that make her anxious. She avoids doctor shows on TV and conversations about illness because they activate her health fears. She avoids watching the news, as well as conversations that involve death or injury, with the hope of not triggering the violent images. And when she can, she tries to avoid social situations, especially interacting with people she doesn't know well. These avoidance behaviors, which are a common way to cope with anxiety, will need to be addressed in subsequent sessions.

When she's in a worried, anxious state, despite her attempts to avoid activating the side screen, she tends to seek out reassurance, especially when worried about her health. She calls her aunt or does research online or visits a medical specialist, hoping to rule out a fatal illness. Ms. J also spends a lot of time—sometimes hours a day—thinking about and analyzing her worries. On other occasions, she tries to push the fear out of her mind by telling herself the worry isn't true or mentally repeating a positive statement: *I'm healthy… I'm healthy.*

Introduction of the Two-Screen Method

After completing the clinical interview, the focus shifts to the treatment plan. I let Ms. J know that we're going to address her anxiety with a new mindfulness-based treatment called the Two-Screen Method. I then describe the two-screen image and method (basically, what you read in chapter 1). I explain that she'll be guided into a new relationship with anxious thoughts and feelings that will cause them to lose their hold on her life. Part of this involves not avoiding, fighting, or watching the side screen. When her internal eyes reflexively go to the anxious content displayed on the side screen, she's to practice redirecting to the front screen, while accepting the anxious threats in her peripheral vision. I let her know that it will take some time to change her relationship with the side screen and that TSM offers tethers to help her maintain focus on the front screen. I walk her through the three anchors on the front screen that will help hold her attention when the anxious side screen is activated: (1) Mindfulness Skills, (2) Healthy Distractions and Activities (HDAs), and (3) Loving Action.

Treatment Goals

After Ms. J has a basic understanding of TSM and how it applies to her anxiety, I hand her a sheet outlining four treatment goals:

- Decrease rumination (watching the side screen), as well as her anxiety/stress level

- Decrease avoidance behaviors (attempts to avoid triggering anxiety)

- Increase mindfulness skills (increase capacity for present-moment awareness)

- Increase healthy, value-based activities (front screen activities)

The first two goals are directed at her relationship with the side screen. In the next ten sessions, she'll work on correcting avoidance behaviors and continually practice the principle of Accept & Redirect, which will protect her from energizing the side screen with the spotlight of attention and reactivity. The last two goals are related to the front screen anchors. In the coming weeks, Ms. J will develop present-moment awareness skills (Mindfulness Skills anchor) and work on implementing healthy, life-giving activities (HDA and Loving Action anchors), especially when feeling anxious. I broadly frame her treatment as gaining freedom from anxiety, while building a more meaningful life. To end our first session together, Ms. J is led through a five-minute focused breathing awareness (FBA) exercise—a mindfulness exercise she'll be practicing daily.

The Second Session

When Ms. J arrives for her session one week later, I'm curious about her experience of applying the two screens. I'm well aware that even if she conceptually understands TSM, it will take time to apply the method. The most challenging part will be responding to the side screen activity with acceptance, not fighting the anxious thoughts and feelings. Ms. J has spent decades reacting and managing her anxiety in a particular way. It will feel unnatural to rotate her attention away from the anxious side screen and not seek reassurance in worried states. It's a complete paradigm shift.

Ms. J reports that having the image of the two screens was helpful during the week. She made a conscious effort not to watch the side screen. She wasn't always successful, but she spent less time investing in anxious thoughts. She describes going out to lunch with a friend who was getting over a cold. Ms. J noticed a funny feeling in her throat and started worrying that she too might get sick. But instead of continuing down this road, Ms. J realized that she was focused on the side screen and ended up redirecting her attention to the conversation. A few minutes later, the fear had passed.

Exposure Therapy for Intrusive Images

The focus of today's session is the intrusive, graphically violent images—such as that of a man bleeding to death—that pop into Ms. J's mind without warning, part of her obsessive anxiety. And it's not just the content that puts Ms. J in a state of alarm. These unwelcome images trigger her fight-or-flight response, so she's instantly flooded with anxiety. Her side screen goes from sleep mode to IMAX theater in a split second. This doesn't give her much time or internal space to thoughtfully respond to the anxiety.

Over the years, these attacking images have taken a toll on her self-concept. She's confused by them. She doesn't understand why her mind would generate content so incongruent with her personality and personal wishes. She wonders what is says about her as a person. At times, she thinks *Maybe deep down I'm a violent person who wishes harm on others* or *Maybe these images are a sign that I'm a bad person.* Because these images are a source of shame and confusion, she has kept them a secret up until now.

I help Ms. J depersonalize the intrusive images and interpret them in a healthy way. We discuss her lack of control over what shows up on the side screen and that the violent content says nothing about her as a person, nor does it indicate any deep wishes. In fact, the images communicate her desire for nonviolence. Anxiety attaches itself to what you care about, what you value in life. The images are so disturbing in part because they violate her values and concern for people's well-being. If she didn't care, there would be no anxious response!

Based on what she's reporting, it's clear Ms. J would benefit from exposure therapy, which effectively decreases the intensity of the content showing up on the side screen. Using the train track analogy presented in chapter 3, I explain how exposure therapy works and why it's important for her to walk toward the fear. We then spend a few minutes listing possible triggers for the violent images. It's similar to the process you went through in chapter 3 to construct your Freedom Ladder, identifying activities that trigger your fear response. On Ms. J's list are things like watching a gory movie, thinking about a car accident, and hearing or saying statements that contain violent themes.

To begin the exposure process, I instruct her to say the phrase, "killed in a car accident." As she mouths these words, an image is triggered, and the side screen lights up. She sees a family mangled in a car accident. Her anxiety shoots up to 85/100. With the side screen blaring, I prompt her to continue saying the statement, while not fighting the image or anxious feeling. It is in this space that her threat center collects new data. I encourage her to hang in there and ride the anxious wave. For the next several minutes her anxiety hovers around 80/100. Then, after nonstop utterances of "killed in a car accident," her anxiety slowly begins to drop. This is a sign that her threat center is learning that violent content is no longer a high-level threat—at least when verbally expressed.

As her anxiety subsides, I direct Ms. J to lean into the present moment (front screen) and hyperfocus on each word I'm saying. This request elevates her anxiety. Even though the violent images are fading on the side screen, she wants to watch and monitor them with her attention. By directing her to shift to the front screen—the present moment, our conversation—I'm asking her to leave the psychological threat unattended on the side screen, which is an unnatural and challenging task for her. I encourage her to rotate her attention away from the side screen and accept the increased sense of vulnerability, as well as the side screen's pull on her mind, as she stays connected to the present moment.

DEBRIEF

As we debrief Ms. J's initial experience of exposure therapy, I highlight the importance of the HDA anchor. When the side screen is activated, her brain will want to study and monitor the anxious content (this is true for all of us). To avoid energizing the side screen and missing out on what is truly important (front screen), she needs to designate in advance specific activities that will hold her attention in anxious moments. For homework, along with practicing FBA, she'll begin working on the HDA anchor.

The Third Session

Ms. J is anxious coming into her session because she knows more exposure therapy is planned. I spend a few minutes reviewing her experiences since last session. She describes a couple of occasions where a violent image came into her mind; however, she found them less jarring than before and was able to move on with her day. What helped was depersonalizing the image—reminding herself that the image wasn't inherently meaningful, nor did it speak to her character.

Recommencing Exposure Therapy

After checking in, we continue with her exposure therapy, which serves two purposes. First, we're undoing the conditioned fear response, where general themes of violence trigger the fight-or-flight response. You want to move toward sources of psychological fears, rather than away, to teach your threat center that the anxious activity may be unpleasant but it's not life-threatening. As you courageously face your fears, you're eventually rewarded with a less active and less intense side screen, as the feared activity stops producing the same anxious discomfort. Second, exposure therapy—and the general idea of moving toward sources of anxiety—offers a training ground, where Ms. J can repeatedly practice the principle of acceptance and the discipline of redirecting attention. Once you become proficient with this step of accepting unwanted thoughts and feelings, while redirecting your attention to the front screen (Accept & Redirect), your life opens up in a new way. You're no longer controlled and overwhelmed by fear. Once you experience this psychological truth, you may start seeking out sources of anxiety, knowing they hold the opportunity for ever-increasing freedom.

To begin, I instruct Ms. J to repeat the statement "killed in a car accident" several times. Images are triggered, but she reports being less rattled and distracted by them. They don't evoke the same level of fear as last week. This is a good sign that the expo-sure therapy from the previous session has taken hold. Her brain has declassified the threat; now she no longer considers verbal statements involving themes of violence a danger to herself.

At this point we don't yet know whether the exposure from last week has generalized to other violent content or applies only to verbal statements concerning violence. We want to make sure her brain understands that seeing violence on TV, for example, or hearing about an accident, just like saying "killed in a car acci-dent" is not deserving of the fight-or-flight response. To ensure that Ms. J's threat center gets the message, we'll continue to provoke the anxious system. Instead of just saying "killed in a car accident," Ms. J will now be exposed to a real car accident caught on video and uploaded to YouTube.

I hit play on the iPad screen and the video begins. Ms. J watches intently as the accident unfolds. Her anxiety spikes after the first run-through. The video is replayed. After she watches the video multiple times, her threat center begins making the adjustment and dials down her anxiety. Debriefing on her experi-ence, she explains that the video did trigger intrusive images, but they were "tolerable." "I'm not as worried about them," she remarks. She expresses being most activated by the sounds of the accident. The thuds. The glass shattering. The screeching of tires.

To explore this further, I rotate the iPad screen away from Ms. J so she's exposed to only the audio. I hit play. About thirty seconds into the clip, I pause the video to get a read on her anxiety. This brief exposure to the audio of the video has signifi-cantly elevated her anxiety, to 75/100. Similar to the previous week, she expresses an overwhelming urge to watch the anxious side screen. Something feels incomplete and unfinished. Her brain wants to create a visual that will make sense of and provide structure for the threatening sounds she's heard. To not have a visual for the car accident feels unsettling and out of control. She has the familiar feeling of not being able to move on with her attention—and her life—until the concern is resolved. I encourage her to lean into the present moment, while accepting the aversive feeling of leaving the side screen content disorganized and unresolved.

Ms. J's experience highlights the role that control can play in your anxious experience. Let's say you're periodically visited by a sense of impending doom, a feeling that something bad is going to happen, or you experience a wave of general insecurity. You won't want to leave the unsettling feeling there in the abstract. You'll want to make sense of it, try to understand it in some way. The fearful, insecure feeling will actively seek out a home. Maybe it gets attached to your professional life—*I'm afraid I'm going to lose all my customers*—or finds its way into your relationships: *I feel like people just pretend to like me but really find me burdensome.* Instead of feeling vulnerable and threatened by something we can't see or touch or know, we give it a name—make the threat more concrete. It's our attempt to contain the emotional vulnerability we feel by tying it to one particular issue—your relationships, your health, your job.

Part of breaking free from anxiety is accepting the feeling of loss of control, allowing the side screen to run its tape without analyzing it or trying to make sense of it. This is hard to do, but the front screen anchors can help. They offer a strong tether for your mind when you feel compelled to impose understanding and control on the side screen content.

Using Healthy Distractions

Wanting Ms. J to practice taking her mind off insecure feelings and unanswered questions, I purposefully distract her after the last exposure exercise. We begin reviewing her preliminary list of HDAs, which include walking the dog or taking a bike ride (physical activities), taking a hot bath or playing the piano (pleasurable activities), and researching her next vacation (general activity). After a few minutes of exploring how she can use the HDA anchor in anxious spaces, she's re-exposed to the crashing sounds on the YouTube video close to a dozen times.

Closing the Session

At the end of session, Ms. J is guided through a brief breath meditation. After the exercise, she reports an anxiety level of 35/100. Her homework for the coming week is to continue practicing focused breathing awareness for ten minutes each day (Mindfulness Skills) and begin experimenting with the HDA anchor in anxious spaces.

The Fourth Session

Ms. J comes into her session and reports several anxious episodes over the last week. She wonders if she's doing something wrong. We explore the difference between the anxious thoughts and feelings that show up on the side screen and her relationship—or set of reactions—to the anxious content. At this point in treatment, she's reminded that progress is not measured by the quantity of anxious thoughts and feelings showing up but rather how she's relating to the anxiety. Ms. J is working on moving into acceptance, while not giving the anxiety her attention on the side screen. Once she's able to consistently apply these principles, her anxiety—robbed of its energy source—will naturally dissipate. She's also reminded that it's not uncommon for anxiety to temporarily increase in the beginning of treatment before it starts going down.

I ask more questions about her experience with anxiety since we last met. She states that it has been hard to keep her eyes off the side screen. She recounts an event that occurred earlier in the week. Shortly after getting a flu vaccination, she heard a news story about a contaminated lot of flu vaccinations discovered on the East Coast. Even though the probability was extremely low, she started worrying that her vaccination was from the contaminated lot. Part of her felt she had a legitimate reason to worry; another part thought she was overreacting. Regardless, she recognized that getting anxious was not helpful, so she tried to redirect her attention away from the anxious side screen. She did her best to apply the Mindfulness Skills anchor and practice present-moment awareness, but her internal eyes kept swiveling back to the side screen.

She expresses frustration that she wasn't able to stay on the front screen and again wonders if she is doing something wrong. I remind her that she's building a new muscle set. When she's in the space of constantly needing to redirect her attention back to the front screen, she's developing this new muscle set. This experience and process of laying down new pathways in the brain will eventually enable her to more easily focus on the object of her choice. I encourage her to be patient with herself and let her know that she's demonstrating good progress.

The Final Round of Exposure to Violent Content

Continuing the exposure therapy from the last two weeks, I replay the car crash video. At this point, the exposure therapy is less focused or concerned with Ms. J's intrusive images. They happen less frequently, and when they do, she doesn't experience the same level of distress. Exposure at this point is mainly directed at the anxiety tied to feeling out of control and not being able to impose order or completeness on an insecure, anxious feeling.

When the video begins (with the screen not visible to Ms. J), she listens intently to screeching tires, glass shattering, and metal warping. She rates her anxiety at 75/100. She listens to the video three more times, and her anxiety drops to 55/100. I continue playing the video. Within ten minutes, the principle of habituation takes hold and her anxiety drops to 30/100, which is considered a subclinical level. I show her my yellow pad, which demonstrates the change in her anxiety ratings. She sees how her anxiety went from 75/100 to 30/100 over the course of fifteen minutes. She's encouraged by the results.

Addressing the Social Anxiety

Over the last four weeks, Ms. J has been making good progress in teaching her threat center not to trigger the fight-or-flight response in response to harmless violent content. Outside the therapy room, she's also been making important gains with her health anxiety—the second branch of her obsessive anxiety. Aside from the recent flu vaccine episode discussed earlier, she's worrying less about health matters and has significantly decreased her avoidance of triggers. She purposefully watched an episode of *ER*, walked into the lobby of a hospital, and didn't shy away from a flu conversation at work. As these and other events activate her side screen, she's diligently applying the first step of TSM, that of Accept & Redirect.

We haven't focused much on her social anxiety; this will now become the primary focus of her treatment. I explain that the quickest and most effective way to tackle the social anxiety is another form of exposure therapy. Currently, she's avoiding social situations where she could be judged or embarrassed, which makes for a very long list. It has gotten to the point where any social interaction holds the potential for her core fear to be realized. To swing the pendulum the other way, she needs to not only break the avoidance pattern but also directly challenge the underlying beliefs that support the social anxiety. She needs to teach her brain that social embarrassment is not dangerous, that it's not worthy of the fight-or-flight response.

This is where the Freedom Ladder can help. In a graduated manner, Ms. J will expose herself to the very kinds of social scenarios that she's been actively protecting against. In other words, she'll purposefully embarrass herself. As I present this idea to Ms. J, you can imagine her internal reaction. *What?* The outlandish nature of the proposed treatment, however, introduces some levity. We both laugh, and she playfully shakes her head at the thought of voluntarily signing up for embarrassment. At the same time, I can tell she sees the value. Something about the approach rings true.

Similar to the process you went through in chapter 3, she identifies various activities that will activate her anxiety at different levels, ranging from 40/100 (mild to moderate anxiety) to 100/100 (the highest level of anxiety). Here's what she came up with:

Freedom Ladder

100/100   Skipping down a busy sidewalk

90/100   Going into a coffee shop and saying, "I'd like a coffee and a corn dog, please"

80/100   "Accidentally" (but purposefully) spilling a cup of water at the food court

70/100   "Accidentally" (but purposefully) dropping papers in a public place

60/100   Going into a coffee shop and asking the staff to explain how they roast coffee

50/100   Returning a purchased item to the store

40/100   Going into a coffee shop and asking to be directed to the restroom

All of these activities are designed to activate her side screen. Each week between sessions, Ms. J will try to complete at least one task from the Freedom Ladder, beginning with the 40/100 activity. As she does, not only will she be recalibrating her fear response, but she'll also be challenging the core assumptions that fuel the social anxiety: that social embarrassment is a cataclysmic event. As she purposefully leads her threat center into the coffee shop and "makes a fool of herself," it will quickly learn that no genuine threat exists. She may feel embarrassed for the moment, but life goes on. She's not shattered by the experience. When the threat center no longer considers the prospect of social embarrassment as a danger, it will turn down the volume on the anxiety.

At the end of the session, Ms. J is assigned the following homework.

- Practice FBA for ten minutes daily and schedule one *mindful driving* and one *washing dishes with mindfulness* exercise in the coming week (Mindfulness Skills anchor).

- Walk into a coffee shop and ask where the restroom is (40/100 on the Freedom Ladder).

- Complete the Compromised Loving Action exercise.

The Fifth Session

Coming into the fifth session, Ms. J reports walking into a coffee shop, approaching the main counter, and asking for directions to the restroom—the first task on the Freedom Ladder. She feared that others would see her as "stupid" because it was "obvious" in her mind where the restroom was. Despite her fears, she went through with the task anyway. She entered the store and without overthinking it, blurted out, "Where's the restroom?" Apparently the employee wasn't surprised by the question and pointed in the direction of the restroom. In recounting the story, it's clear Ms. J feels a sense of victory, as she should.

For the remainder of the session, we go through her results of the Compromised Loving Action exercise and explore how Ms. J might implement the Loving Action anchor. The loving behaviors most suppressed by her anxiety are *service, availability, spirituality*, and *generosity*. These expressions of self are deeply important to her, and she feels the loss when anxiety interferes with living them out. We spend time going through each loving action, as you did in chapter 8, clearly defining what each one looks like in terms of concrete, behavioral actions. For example, one expression of *generosity* for Ms. J is giving her time to an elderly grandparent, whether that's a personal visit or a phone call. And *availability* is defined as the act of deep listening to others and reflecting, in the moment, how she can be a supportive presence in the relationship. Through this process, she created a menu of behaviors—specific loving actions—that she could pursue in the presence of an active side screen.

Homework

- Repeat the mindful driving and dishwashing exercises, as well as maintain the FBA practice.

- Complete an activity on the Freedom Ladder for her social anxiety.

- Look for an opportunity to apply the Loving Action anchor.

The Sixth Session

Ms. J walks in and tells me, "It has been a good week." There has been a shift. During the week there were several times when the anxious side screen lit up and she felt under threat. But each time she was able to move into at least partial emotional acceptance and find an alternative home for her mind (front screen anchor). When she applied Accept & Redirect and took advantage of one of the front screen anchors, she noticed that after a few minutes the anxious worry felt less important and intense.

She also experimented with the Loving Action anchor. Earlier in the week a stomach pain generated a fear of cancer. She would typically call a family member for reassurance or research her symptoms online. Instead, she reviewed her list of loving actions and acted on one of the expressions of *service*. Usually serving others was the last thing on her mind when feeling under threat. But she called the outreach coordinator of a local animal shelter that has been on her radar, inquiring about volunteer opportunities. Taking this step felt empowering to Ms. J. She didn't let the anxiety compromise an important value. She didn't allow the fear of terminal illness to block her from being the person she wanted to be. In fact, she used the anxiety as a catalyst for purposeful action. And staying true to the ideal expression of self had the added benefit of keeping her attention off the side screen.

Grounding Skills

To complete the Mindfulness Skills anchor, Ms. J needs to be introduced to one additional exercise. You may recall from chapter 4 the grounding technique, which functions as an emotional reset button when you find yourself overwhelmed and overpowered by the side screen. Grounding pops you out of the narrative-focus network in your brain—the place where you're stuck and being emotionally flooded—and guides you into the experiential-focus network, which offers mental awareness and the experience of self in the present moment. To help Ms. J become familiar with and practice this important skill, I direct her to listen intently to all the sounds she can detect in the room. She observes how her body feels on the couch and the pressure of her feet against the floor. She visually studies a piece of art hanging on the wall and carefully inhales the aroma of a tea bag I hand to her. As you did in chapter 4, she practices the skill of hyperfocusing on different aspects of the present moment with her five senses.

Homework

- Practice the grounding exercise, the breath meditation, as well as approaching everyday tasks with the intention of mindfulness (Mindfulness Skills anchor).

- Continue practicing Accept & Redirect, followed by the implementation of one or more of the front screen anchors.

- Complete two more activities on the Freedom Ladder (social anxiety).

The Seventh Session

The session begins with an overview of Ms. J's week and her general experience with anxiety. She reports a significant decrease in intrusive images. And when they do show up, she comments, "I'm not that bothered by them anymore." This is a good sign that the exposure therapy has done its job and is holding. Her brain no longer responds to innocuous violent themes or images with the fight-or-flight response. Instead of the intrusive images being a source of extreme distress and private shame, they've been downgraded to a nuisance that doesn't spoil the moment or her day.

We then shift to her social anxiety. Over the last several weeks she has been steadily climbing the Freedom Ladder. She expresses being most challenged by anticipatory anxiety—the anxiety that comes with anticipating an upcoming event. This is not surprising, because anticipatory anxiety is often higher and more torturous than the anxiety generated by the actual feared event. Fear of the unknown, fueled by our imagination and what-if's, is a well-known source of anxious worry. One to two days before a Freedom Ladder activity, Ms. J reports a steady stream of anxious thoughts. "I think about wasting people's time...others thinking I'm stupid...coming across as rude...all sorts of stuff," she says. On multiple occasions in the past week she caught herself hanging out with these thoughts on the side screen. At times, when she was trying to keep her attention off the side screen, it felt as if the fear were stalking her, ready to pounce and overwhelm her at any moment.

To help defuse the anticipatory anxiety, I make a suggestion for the coming week. When the anticipatory anxiety shows up, she's to stop and ask herself, *What's the hardest thing to accept right now?* and *What am I most afraid of right now?* After she identifies the core fear, she's to practice radical acceptance, saying to herself, *I can live with that possibility* [whatever the threat is] and *I can live with this feeling right now.* By taking this bold step toward acceptance, she'll likely experience a significant decrease in anticipatory anxiety. In addition, by creating emotional space for the worst-case scenario—essentially feeling the source of anxiety in advance—the actual activity will carry less of an anxious charge, as she will have accepted and partially metabolized it in advance.

The Eighth Session

Ms. J comes in and describes her experiences with the Freedom Ladder activities. How she did this past week will be revealing. She was taking on a major challenge. The plan was to have lunch at her local food court and at some point purposefully spill a glass of water. This activity, which we thought would generate an 80/100 anxiety level, would be embarrassing even for people who don't suffer from social anxiety, as it would draw lots of curious looks and attention from the surrounding tables. For Ms. J, the prospect of spilling water in public was unthinkable. It cut right to a core fear. Even thinking about it made her cringe. But, as she says, "I knew I needed to go through with it." She was tired of being controlled by the anxiety, and she saw the benefit of these "crazy" Freedom Ladder activities. In fact, she noticed that her relationship to anxiety was changing. Overall, she was less anxious than she used to be, and she found herself being more assertive in a variety of contexts. Recognizing these gains, she knew she couldn't stop now. She was determined to spill the water.

As the day approached, she experienced waves of anticipatory anxiety. This time she was careful not to watch the side screen, and she repeatedly told herself, *I can live with this feeling.* When she practiced accepting the anxious idea scrolling across the side screen, the fear seemed to fade into the background after a few minutes. She repeatedly told herself not to fight the feeling while putting her mind on something else. On one occasion, she applied the HDA anchor by researching different cruise liners for an upcoming family vacation.

On the day of "Operation Spill Water," she was nervous. She didn't know what to expect. On the drive to the shopping mall, her anxiety level was around 50/100, which surprised her a little.

She had thought it would be higher. Her anxiety stayed at this level as she parked and made her way to the food court. With a slice of pizza and large ice water on her tray, she found a table in the center of the food court. After a couple of minutes, she took a deep breath and pushed over the water cup. Water flooded the table and spilled onto the floor. Her anxiety shot up to 80/100. Several people took notice, and a young child even pointed. Ms. J, who came prepared, discreetly pulled out the rag she'd brought and began cleaning up the mess. She then ate her lunch and began reading the newspaper, which was part of the assignment; we had wanted her to practice using a healthy distraction after the initial exposure. She tried to focus on the newspaper but found herself highly distracted. The side screen was vying for her attention. She wanted to think about what had happened and how she was being perceived. She kept redirecting her attention to the front screen—in this case, the front-page article. Over the next several minutes her anxiety gradually subsided. Twenty minutes later she left the mall and felt a sense of victory. She had faced one of her biggest fears and survived. "It wasn't as bad as I thought," she tells me with a smile.

I congratulate Ms. J and encourage her to maintain the momentum. During the next week Ms. J plans to do a social activity that she expects will raise her anxiety to 90/100. She's to walk into her local coffee shop and order a corn dog. This activity is more anxiety provoking than the others, because it's "obvious" that the place doesn't serve corn dogs. Spilling water is a clumsy act, while ordering a corn dog at a coffee shop is a "stupid" act in her mind. She wonders out loud if she can go through with it. She feels more resistance to doing this activity than to any of the other interventions we've done to date. I begin working with her on letting go and softening around the underlying fear. After a few minutes of exercising the acceptance muscle, we review how she may be challenged by the anxious side screen in the coming week and how she can use one or more of the front screen anchors to help. For homework, she plans on completing the Loving Action Assessment.

The Ninth Session

During the past week Ms. J completed the Freedom Ladder. She went into the coffee place and ordered a corn dog. She laughs when describing the insanity of doing such a thing. She got hit with an anxious spike when walking into the store and uttering the words. She says, "Even though my anxiety went through the roof, I was still able to stay anchored and engaged with what I was doing." After requesting a corn dog (and politely being told, with a smile, that they don't serve corn dogs), she purposefully stayed in the store until her anxiety dropped to a level of 40/100.

In the following days, when she was tempted to ruminate and review the corn dog incident, she used either healthy distractions or loving actions to keep her mind off the side screen. On one occasion she caught herself worrying about who had been present in the coffee shop when she tried to order a corn dog. She feared that someone she knew might have been there. Instead of staying with the anxious thoughts, she picked up the phone and called a good friend from college with whom she'd lost touch, which represented a radically different coping strategy. The corn dog event left Ms. J feeling insecure—especially socially. When she walked out of the coffee shop, she felt as if "FOOL" were written across her forehead for all the world to see. In this insecure space, the last thing she wanted to do was interact with others, especially a long-lost friend. She didn't feel like herself and was afraid her fears of being seen as foolish would be confirmed. Despite these insecure feelings, she did the unnatural and reached out to her college friend. She allowed her values to lead instead of the anxious feeling.

For the balance of the session we review TSM and how she's applying it to her social anxiety and health fears. We take this time to fill in any gaps in either her understanding or her application of Accept & Redirect, as well as her use of the front screen anchors. We explore possible HDA anchors that could invite more aliveness into her life (enlivening activities), as well as talk through how she plans to cultivate the loving behaviors identified in the Loving Action Assessment (chapter 8).

The Tenth Session

When we began treatment, Ms. J and I had agreed to meet for ten sessions, with the possibility of follow-up sessions if needed. Today is the tenth session.

Originally, Ms. J's last task on the Freedom Ladder was going to be skipping down a public sidewalk. In the previous session we agreed that "ordering a corn dog at a coffee shop" would be the final activity. Even though it was originally designated a 90/100 activity, her anxiety actually reached a 100/100 during the exercise, a level that typically correlates with the last activity on the Freedom Ladder, and she has consistently demonstrated a willingness and ability to confront her social fears. And she's considerably less anxious. She's less preoccupied with what people think, and she's consistently finding her voice in a variety of ways. As evidence for this shift, Ms. J recounts a recent dining experience where she reminded the waiter of a missing drink order. This caught the attention of a family member, who even commented on the change. Ms. J and I both feel confident that she is on a path to more freedom socially and that the formality of the Freedom Ladder was no longer necessary. As long as she doesn't fall back into an avoidance pattern and continues to apply TSM, the social anxiety will continue to dissipate.

I ask Ms. J how she feels about her progress. She hesitates and says, "Pretty good." As is often the case with anxiety, or any area of growth for that matter, it's easy to forget how much has changed. I pull out the sheet from the first session, which outlines the goals of treatment:

- Decrease rumination (watching the side screen), as well as her anxiety/stress level

- Decrease avoidance behaviors (attempts to avoid triggering anxiety)

- Increase mindfulness skills (increase capacity for present-moment awareness)

- Increase healthy, value-based activities (front screen activities)

As we start going through each goal, the gains are clear. Ms. J no longer feels attacked by violent, intrusive images, and when they do show up, which is infrequently, they quickly dissipate because of her nonreactive response. Over the last ten weeks she has faced her social fears head-on, putting herself in potentially embarrassing social situations that would have seemed unthinkable prior to treatment. This brave action dispelled a lot of the assumptions that fueled Ms. J's social fears. It also changed the scale for what was considered hard. The stuff she used to worry about socially was nothing compared to spilling water in public or ordering a corn dog at a coffee shop. But most important, there has been a fundamental change in how she relates to anxiety. Whether it's responding to health fears or purposefully triggering the side screen with the Freedom Ladder, she has learned how to respond to anxiety in a new way. By using TSM, she learned how to accept anxious feelings, while placing the precious resource of attention on the front screen. She also discovered that she could take the anxious energy being kicked off the side screen and use it for actions and activities that moved her life forward.

With all these gains, Ms. J's life is not perfect, nor is it free of anxiety. In fact, in this final session she reports tossing and turning the previous night due to work-related stress. At the same time, she indicates that her baseline anxiety—her average level of anxiety experienced most days—is in the 40/100 range. This is a significant decrease from the 65/100 to 80/100 anxiety level she reported ten weeks ago. With a smile, she observes that when she does experience an anxious episode, "I guess it's another opportunity to practice acceptance."

We discuss the importance of continuing to exercise the acceptance and nonresistance muscle when the side screen is activated. We also review the three anchors on the front screen, paying special attention to those techniques and activities that have been most effective in keeping her eyes tethered to the front screen. She's encouraged to continue practicing FBA and other mindfulness exercises to keep her stress levels low. We also high-light the importance of not letting internal tension or an anxious feeling block her from freely living her life.

After summarizing the major themes of treatment and cele-brating the courageous steps she's taken toward mental and emo-tional freedom, we say our goodbyes and schedule a follow-up session for several months later.

Hopefully, Ms. J's case has given you more clarity and confi-dence in applying TSM to your own life. While the particulars of your anxious experience and worries may be different than Ms. J's, you'll want to apply the same steps and principles outlined in this chapter. Regardless of what shows up on your side screen, the pathway to freedom is accepting the presence of the hard thoughts and feelings (Accept & Redirect), while finding a safe home for your mental attention that enhances your quality of life (using the front screen anchors).

As we enter the final leg of our journey together, let's address any lingering questions you might have about TSM and its appli-cation—the subject of the next chapter.

CHAPTER 10

Q&A FROM THE COUCH
Common Questions and Experiences

For close to ten years, I've been actively using the Two-Screen Method in my clinical practice, as well as training other mental health professionals in the method. As clients begin applying the method, they have many of the same questions for me. As you've been reading this book, I suspect you too have had some questions. I hope that, along the way, most of your questions have been answered. The goal of this brief chapter is to address any questions you may still have, so you can use TSM with full confidence and benefit.

Where should I start, in terms of applying the Two-Screen Method?

The best place to start is catching yourself watching the side screen and practicing the art of redirection—redirecting your internal eyes and attention to the front screen. Over time, you want to spend less and less time on the side screen, which requires you to increase awareness of what you're doing internally—what you're thinking about and where your attention is. It can be helpful to pause several times during the day and ask the question, *Where is my mind right now?* If you find yourself entertaining a worry or drifting with a depressing thought, bring your mind into the present moment (Mindfulness Skills anchor) or employ one of the other front screen anchors (Healthy Distractions and Activities and Loving Action).

In addition, it's important that you have a detailed profile of what shows up on your side screen. If worry or anxiety is the main issue, make sure you complete the exercise in chapter 2, Understanding Your Anxious Side Screen. You want to clearly identify the types of thoughts, feelings, images, and physical sensations that show up on your side screen. This will allow you to see side screen activation more quickly and help you discern between side screen content—recurring worries and destructive moods—and legitimate concerns (issues that require immediate attention and problem solving) and healthy emotional experiences, such as natural feelings of loss, that are part of living a productive and meaningful life.

What should I expect, in terms of positive change, as I begin applying TSM?

Most practitioners of TSM tend to follow a familiar pattern. Initially, there is a sense of relief and hope in understanding your internal experience and having a clear plan to change the current pattern. Even though your struggle is not immediately resolved, you can see the problem—side screen—and the solution: allowing the side screen to be present in your internal world while tethering your mind to the front screen.

In the initial days of practicing TSM, many clients report spending less time watching the side screen, which equates to spending less time worrying or indulging the unhealthy desires that fuel bad habits (addictive side screen). However, especially in the first month of applying the method, it's also common to encounter certain challenges. First, you may find it difficult to keep your attention off the side screen. Despite your continued efforts to redirect back to the front screen, you may find yourself back in the same space—gazing at the worries scrolling across the side screen. This is to be expected. The side screen can exert a strong pull on your mind. The key is to stay patient and committed to redirecting your attention to the front screen over and over again. This is part of the training—the process of renewing your mind. You're building a new muscle set. Combined with your mindfulness training (Mindfulness Skills anchor), this act of redirecting will—over time—increase your capacity to focus on the object of your choosing. In other words, with practice you'll find it easier to stay on the front screen when distracting thoughts and feelings get kicked up. But first you need to develop the muscle set, which you're doing each time you catch yourself watching the side screen and rotate your internal eyes back to the front screen.

The second common struggle is finding an alternative home for your mind that isn't the side screen. After removing your eyes from the side screen, there will be times when you're not sure where to go with your attention and life energy. This is to be expected, because in the beginning you're not well acquainted with the front screen anchors, which are designed for this express purpose. They provide an anchor for your mind when the side screen is vying for your attention. But you must devote some time and effort to eventually take full advantage of these front-screen tethers. Conceptually, they are easy to understand, such as keeping your mind in the present moment or engaging in a healthy distraction. But to make them useful, especially in challenging emotional spaces, you need to go beyond a cursory understanding and application. It's not enough to remind yourself to engage in a healthy distraction or practice present-moment awareness in the midst of an anxious experience or intense craving. During these vulnerable times, you need the benefit of the mindfulness training outlined in chapter 4. You will need a clear plan and designated activities to pursue in these critical spaces—a comprehensive strategy addressed in chapter 6 (Healthy Distractions and Activities anchor). In short, to gain the mental and emotional freedom you seek, carefully read the chapters on the front screen anchors and implement the suggested exercises.

Depending on the severity of your particular symptoms, if you fully dedicate yourself to the material in this book, you will likely experience a significant decrease in anxious thoughts and feelings after approximately twelve weeks. Again, this varies from person to person. I've had clients experience a breakthrough using TSM after only one or two training sessions—a pleasantly surprising but rare result. I've also had clients on the other end, who've taken longer to see an appreciable difference in their anxiety level. This is a good segue into the next common question: what do you do when, after a consistent effort in applying TSM, you still find yourself struggling? Aside from continuing your own personal therapy (which remains highly recommended), if you continue to be overwhelmed and don't notice a positive change after twelve weeks, you may want to consider taking medication.

Do people take medication in combination with TSM?

All side screens are not created equal. Your side screen may be the equivalent of an IMAX theater with Dolby surround sound, routinely overwhelming you with worries and anxious feelings. If this describes your experience, even after applying TSM and practicing mindfulness for several months, you may want to consider one of the mainline psychotropics, such as an SSRI or SNRI, as a way of turning down the volume on your side screen. By reducing the intensity of your anxious experience, you may find yourself in a better position to apply and benefit from the steps laid out in this book.

Keep in mind, medication doesn't have to be a long-term solution. Clients in my practice who elect to take medication often do so on a short-term basis, maybe six to twelve months, to jump-start the change process. They view medication as a bridge that helps them travel from where they are now to where they want to be—to mental and emotional freedom. Once they realize their therapeutic goals, they reassess—under the prescriber's guidance and supervision—their need for medication.

Can I integrate TSM into my current therapy?

TSM is a flexible mindfulness-based treatment that can be used on its own or in conjunction with other therapies or change programs. At its core, TSM is a user-friendly way of defusing problematic thoughts and feelings, which gives it broad applicability. You can fold it into other mindfulness-based treatments, such as acceptance and commitment therapy (ACT) or mindfulness-based stress reduction (MBSR), bolstering your ability to apply the recommended strategies in these approaches. You can also incorporate TSM in therapies that are outside the cognitive-behavioral or mindfulness-based framework, such as psychodynamic therapies, which focus on relating current symptoms to formative experiences from your past. All therapeutic approaches, regardless of their theoretical orientation and approach to change, share the goal of relieving unnecessary suffering. Having an easy way to de-energize unhelpful thoughts and feelings, which TSM offers, should be welcome and compatible with all forms of therapy. TSM doesn't need to compete or conflict with the therapeutic work you're currently doing. It can help support your change process regardless of your therapist's orientation.

If you're in therapy, I would discuss TSM with your therapist and explore how it could be used in and out of session to support your personal growth and healing. As you raise the issue, it's important to highlight that TSM is a platform for applying mindfulness principles, especially in emotionally charged spaces. Emphasizing this point will clarify for your therapist what TSM is and how it can be incorporated into your work together.

Is mindfulness (the Two-Screen Method) compatible with my faith?

When working with religious clients or speaking in church settings, I occasionally get questions about mindfulness and its associations with Buddhism. People question whether mindfulness, both its principles and its practices—such as not resisting a jealous feeling or worrisome thoughts (the principle of acceptance), or engaging in a breath meditation, a common practice in Buddhism—is congruent with their spiritual beliefs. When these concerns are raised, I share my belief that mindfulness, as it's practiced in the field of psychology, is not only compatible with faith but is also a valuable resource for increasing spiritual awareness in daily life, as well as your ability to live out the ideals of your faith tradition. Let me explain.

Your internal world, much like the physical world, is governed by a set of natural laws. In the external world, for example, there is the law of gravity—an object tossed into the air follows a predictable path. Your internal world also obeys a set of rules and principles. Certain mental and emotional actions energize internal sensations (thoughts, feelings, and physical sensations), while others cause them to dissipate. We've learned that an internal disposition of mindfulness, a posture of acceptance and nonresistance, removes the power of negative internal forces. In this respect, mindfulness is an important ally that can support and even enhance your spiritual journey and faith-based life.

This is one reason why many faith traditions have practices to cultivate the equivalent of mindfulness. It just goes under different names. The Christian faith, for example, has a rich history of meditation and other spiritual disciplines that resemble mindfulness, from St. Francis of Assisi and other monastics to St. Teresa of Avila and St. John of the Cross, who practiced the discipline of present-moment awareness in an effort to more fully experience God's presence. Today a few examples of mindfulness-like practices are Lectio Divina, contemplative prayer and scriptural reading, and Sarah Young's bestselling devotional, *Jesus Calling*, which actively integrates mindfulness principles.

Mindfulness, like prayer, is merely a vehicle. What is important is the intention of the driver and the ultimate destination of the vehicle. Millions of people, in this very moment, are praying all around the world. Knowing that people are praying doesn't tell us much. We don't know why they're praying or the belief system supporting this activity. Some of these prayers may be to God or a higher power. Others may not. Some of these prayers may carry loving intent and blessings to others. Others may not. What matters is the heart and intention of the people praying. Prayer, like mindfulness, is just a vehicle. We are the ones who assign meaning, purpose, and intent to the given activity, not the other way around.

Following this line of thought, both a Buddhist and a Christian can be engaged in a breath meditation, following and focusing solely on the breath. While the exercise may look the same from the outside, the goals and meanings they attach to the exercise are different. During the breath meditation, the Buddhist may be reminded of the self being an illusion and the importance of detaching from sensory experience. The Christian or Jewish practitioner, on the other hand, may be reminded of the scripture where God "breathed into his [Adam's] nostrils the breath of life, and the man became a living being" (Genesis 2:7). Framed in this way, the breath is followed with an openness to God's presence and a spirit of gratitude for being granted the breath of life. Thus the intention of the practitioner can change the meaning and function of the same mindfulness exercise.

In summary, the Two-Screen Method—and its application of mindfulness—offers a natural platform for spiritual integration. The cultivation of present-moment awareness can go hand in hand with a deeper experience of the divine. And the development of mindfulness skills can help you have more control over your day-to-day behavior, increasing your capacity to more fully live out the values contained in your spiritual beliefs.

Where do I go from here, after I've read this book?

The first careful reading of this book will give you a solid foundation for the internal steps that lead to mental and emotional freedom. From there, you need to practice—and continue to practice—the TSM steps of Accept & Redirect (step one), while tethering your mind to the front screen with one or more of the front screen anchors (step two). As you engage diligently in this practice, you'll likely benefit from rereading those sections of the book most related to your struggle. If worry and anxiety are your main issues, you may want to read chapters 2 and 3 several times. There is a lot of information packed into these chapters. With each read-through something new may stand out to you or you may more deeply internalize a helpful concept. The same is true for issues related to the addictive side screen (destructive patterns of behavior) and depressive side screen (negative mood states). Revisiting the chapters dedicated to each of these side screens can reinforce what you've already learned and help you make important refinements in how you apply TSM.

You may also find yourself underutilizing one or more of the front screen anchors. If you're not applying the Loving Action anchor or taking full advantage of Healthy Distractions and Activities, for example, reread these chapters and make it a goal to incorporate them into your daily or weekly life for the next month.

Last, and most important, stay committed to mindfulness training. Practice the exercises outlined in chapter 4; use other resources to cultivate this important discipline. The more you expand your mindfulness muscle set, the easier you will find it to apply the Two-Screen Method and gain the freedom you desire.

CONCLUSION

We began our journey with a simple truth that's easy to miss: *You have a relationship with thoughts and feelings.* There are the thoughts that come into your mind and the things you feel, and then there is your relationship to this internal activity—your set of responses to it. When a worry pops into your mind or you're hit with an anxious feeling, you are free to respond in a variety of ways. You have choices in terms of your attitude or internal disposition toward the challenge, where you decide to invest your mental attention, and the behavioral choices you make; for example, *Driving into the city makes me anxious. Should I play it safe and stay home, or should I go to my friend's birthday dinner?*

When you're feeling good and free of worries, you don't need to give much thought to how you relate to your internal world. Making the distinction between your core self and the surrounding thoughts and feelings you experience doesn't carry much significance. You just think, feel, and freely live your life. Where the problem occurs—where your relationship to inner activity really matters—is when challenging thoughts and feelings show up. In this situation, if you don't take specific mental and emotional steps—steps that are counterintuitive and need to be learned—you're in danger of being consumed by worrisome thoughts and anxious feelings and other threats to your well-being.

In this book, you were introduced to a method that guides you into the ideal relationship with worries and destructive moods, so these and other barriers to happiness dissipate from your life. The Two-Screen Method equips you with an image that naturally separates your internal world into a front screen and side screen. The front screen is your experience of the present moment, as well as the home of life-giving and meaningful thoughts, feelings, and images—all that inner activity associated with a full, vibrant life. Then off to the right there is a side screen. This is where your worries and anxious feelings and other threats to your well-being show up. The method then guides you through the change process by having you relate to each screen as directed.

In chapters 2, 3, 5, and 7 you explored the three main types of side screens (anxious side screen, addictive side screen, and depressive side screen), including the importance of applying the universal principle of Accept & Redirect, with each side screen type having its own particular priority and emphasis within this directive. With the *anxious side screen*, the goal is to accept the psychological experience of being under threat—the sense that something important to you is at risk—followed by the unnatural step of taking your internal eyes off the perceived concern displayed on the side screen. With the *addictive side screen*, the highest priority is avoiding seduction by quickly redirecting your attention away from the unhealthy enticement. Yet acceptance is still important and needed. It's about letting go and accepting the mental, emotional, and physiological experience of not satisfying a craving or an urge. Lastly, the primary task with the *depressive side screen* is catching yourself investing in depressive thought patterns (side screen) and making the firm commitment to move outward with your attention and life energy. This requires you to act with purpose when you don't feel like it—when the motivation to change your mood and life for the better is absent. It involves accepting the experience of engaging life and others when you feel weighed down, joyless, and skeptical that the given activity offers any value or benefit.

Woven in between these side screen chapters were the front screen anchors, which are designed for two purposes: (1) to protect you from energizing the side screen with your attention and (2) to improve your quality of life. In chapter 4, you were introduced to the Mindfulness Skills anchor and encouraged to regularly practice a set of mindfulness exercises. Practices such as focused breathing awareness and grounding skills will increase your capacity for present-moment awareness—an outcome associated with well-being—and decrease the power and presence of the side screen in your life. In chapter 6, you learned how the Healthy Distractions and Activities anchor can provide a healthy home for your attention and life energy, while moving your life forward in a positive way, whether that's increasing healthy living or injecting more aliveness into your life. In chapter 8 you explored the third front screen anchor, that of Loving Action. Accordingly, in the midst of your struggle, you're presented with an opportunity to do something deeply meaningful—something that you likely don't often consider. You can focus on loving others. You can use your worries and anxious energy as a catalyst to positively influence their lives. When you use the side screen—which has been a source of pain and problems in your life—to express the best parts of who you are, there is the ultimate sense of victory and contentment.

My hope is that you've benefited from the ideas shared in this book and that you diligently practice the Two-Screen Method. If you do, I'm confident you'll experience the mental and emotional freedom I've observed in the lives of my clients, as well as in my own life. If you stay the course, I believe you'll draw closer to becoming the person you were wired to be. As St. Irenaeus of Lyons said, in the words that open this book, "The Glory of God is the human person fully alive."

Taking this journey with you has been a privilege.

ACKNOWLEDGMENTS

The road to writing and publishing this book has been a long one—a journey I didn't take alone. Every step of the way my loving wife, Melissa Symington, was there listening to my ideas, reading chapters, offering helpful feedback, and encouraging me when I needed it the most. On countless occasions, she sacrificed her own needs in our young family of two children (Samuel and Naomi), to give me protected space to write. Her commitment to me and this book was tireless and invaluable. From the bottom of my heart, I love you and thank you.

I also want to express my gratitude to New Harbinger Publications, beginning with the acquisitions editor Jess O'Brien, who believed in the project and helped me sharpen the book's focus to ensure that it would reach the intended audience and have maximum impact. From there, I had the privilege of working with a team of gifted editors. One editor in particular, Vicraj Gill, was with me throughout the developmental and copyediting process. In her positive style, Vicraj helped me structure the book and refine my writing style to be more clear, engaging, and concise. My experience with New Harbinger was nothing but positive and rewarding.

Lastly, bringing this book to fruition was a test of commitment and perseverance. I want to thank my parents (Mom and Gerry; Dad and Ann), as well as Cliff and Joyce Penner, for modeling these traits and walking with me on this book journey. Your lives demonstrate that through hard work, faith, and a good sense of humor, dreams are possible.

REFERENCES

Althof, S. E. 2010. "What's New in Sex Therapy?" *Journal of Sexual Medicine* 7: 5–13.

Beck, A. T., A. J. Rush, B. F. Shaw, and G. Emery. 1979. *Cognitive Therapy of Depression*. New York: Guilford.

Burns, D. D. 1980. *Feeling Good: The New Mood Therapy*. New York: William Morrow.

Carson, J. K., K. M. Carson, K. M. Gil, and D. H. Baucom. 2004. "Mindfulness-Based Relationship Enhancement." *Behavior Therapy* 35, 3: 471–494.

Farb, N. A. S., Z. S. Segal, H. Mayberg, J. Bean, D. McKeon, Z. Fatima, and A. K. Anderson. 2007. "Attending to the Present: Mindfulness Meditation Reveals Distinct Neural Modes of Self-Reference." *Scan* 2: 313–322.

Forsyth, J. P., and G. H. Eifert. 2016. *The Mindfulness and Acceptance Workbook for Anxiety: A Guide to Breaking Free from Anxiety, Phobias, and Worry Using Acceptance and Commitment Therapy*. 2nd ed. Oakland, CA: New Harbinger.

Hayes, S. C., J. B. Luoma, F. W. Bond, A. L. Masuda, and J. Lillis. 2006. "Acceptance and Commitment Therapy: Model, Processes, and Outcomes." *Behavior Research and Therapy* 44: 1–25.

Hayes, S. C., and S. Smith. 2005. *Get Out of Your Mind and Into Your Life: The New Acceptance and Commitment Therapy*. Oakland, CA: New Harbinger.

Hoffman, S. G., A. T. Sawyer, A. A. Witt, and D. Oh. 2010. "The Effect of Mindfulness-Based Therapy on Anxiety and Depression: A Meta-Analytic Review." *Journal of Consulting and Clinical Psychology* 78: 169–183.

Juarascio, A. S., E. M. Forman, and J. D. Herbert. 2010. "Acceptance and Commitment Therapy vs. Cognitive Therapy for the Treatment of Comorbid Eating Pathology." *Behavior Modification* 34: 175–190.

Kabat-Zinn, J. 1990. *Full Catastrophe Living: Using the Wisdom of Your Body and Mind to Face Stress, Pain, and Illness.* New York: Bantam Dell.

———. 1994. *Wherever You Go, There You Are: Mindfulness Meditation in Everyday Life.* New York: Hyperion.

———. 2013. *Full Catastrophe Living: Using the Wisdom of Your Body and Mind to Face Stress, Pain, and Illness.* Rev. ed. New York: Bantam Dell.

Kabat-Zinn, J., A. O. Massion, J. Kristeller, et al. 1992. "Effectiveness of a Meditation-Based Stress Reduction Program in the Treatment of Anxiety Disorders." *American Journal of Psychiatry* 149: 936–943.

Kleim, D., C. Kröger, and J. Kosfelder. 2010. "Dialectical Behavior Therapy for Borderline Personality Disorder: A Meta-Analysis Using Mixed-Effects Modeling." *Journal of Consulting and Clinical Psychology* 78: 936–951.

Kristeller, J. L., and C. B. Hallett. 1999. "An Exploratory Study of a Meditation-Based Intervention for Binge Eating Disorders." *Journal of Health Psychology* 4: 357–363.

Langer, E. J., and M. Moldoveanu. 2000. "The Construct of Mindfulness." *Journal of Social Issues* 56: 1–9.

Linehan, M. M. 1993. *Cognitive-Behavioral Treatment of Borderline Personality Disorder.* New York: Guilford Press.

Ost, L. G. 2008. "Efficacy of the Third Wave of Behavioral Therapies: A Systematic Review and Meta-Analysis." *Behavior Research and Therapy* 46: 296–321.

PSYCHALIVE: Psychology for Everyday Life. n.d. "How You Can Change Your Brain." https://www.psychalive.org/how-you-can-change-your-brain.

Segal, Z. V., J. M. G. Williams, and J. D. Teasdale. 2002. *Mindfulness-Based Cognitive Therapy for Depression*. New York: Guilford Press.

Speca, M., L. E. Carlson, E. Goodey, and M. Angen. 2000. "A Randomized, Wait-List Controlled Clinical Trial: The Effect of a Mindfulness Meditation-Based Stress Reduction Program on Mood and Symptoms of Stress in Cancer Outpatients." *Psychosomatic Medicine* 62: 613–622.

Stahl, B., and E. Goldstein. 2010. *A Mindfulness-Based Stress Reduction Workbook*. Oakland, CA: New Harbinger.

Twohig, M. P., S. C. Hayes, J. C. Plumb, L. D. Pruitt, A. B. Collins, H. Hazlett-Stevens, et al. 2010. "A Randomized Clinical Trial of Acceptance and Commitment Therapy vs. Progressive Relaxation Training for Obsessive Compulsive Disorder." *Journal of Consulting and Clinical Psychology* 78: 705–716.

VIA Institute on Character. n.d. http://www.viacharacter.org.

Scott Symington, PhD, is a clinical psychologist who is dedicated to helping adults overcome worry and anxiety, negative moods, addictive behaviors, and other conditions stealing people's joy and freedom. In addition to a full-time private practice, he regularly speaks at professional conferences; large church groups; graduate schools and universities; and business groups, including the Young Presidents' Organization (YPO). Symington earned a PhD in clinical psychology from the Fuller Graduate School of Psychology, and completed an MA in theology from Fuller Theological Seminary. His career path began in the business and consulting world. Then in 1998, after much soul searching, he decided to leave a lucrative position brokering agricultural products to pursue his true passion: clinical psychology—a profession that lined up with both his head and heart.

One of his primary interests, which is informed by his diverse experiences and training, is making the evidence-based methods of psychology and spiritual wisdom easy to understand and easy to apply to your daily life. Symington practices and resides in Pasadena, CA.

Register your **new harbinger** titles for additional benefits!

When you register your **new harbinger** title—purchased in any format, from any source—you get access to benefits like the following:

- Downloadable accessories like printable worksheets and extra content

- Instructional videos and audio files

- Information about updates, corrections, and new editions

Not every title has accessories, but we're adding new material all the time.

Access free accessories in 3 easy steps:

1. Sign in at NewHarbinger.com (or **register** to create an account).

2. Click on **register a book**. Search for your title and click the **register** button when it appears.

3. Click on the **book cover or title** to go to its details page. Click on **accessories** to view and access files.

That's all there is to it!

If you need help, visit:

NewHarbinger.com/accessories

new harbinger
CELEBRATING
40 YEARS